VIRGINIA TEST PREP
Revising and Editing
Practice Workbook
Grade 4

© 2018 by V. Hawas

All rights reserved. No part of this book may be reproduced or transmitted in any form or by any means, electronic, mechanical, photocopying, recording, or otherwise without prior written permission.

ISBN 978-1725883826

TEST MASTER PRESS

www.testmasterpress.com

CONTENTS

Introduction	**4**
Revising and Editing Practice Sets	**5**
Passage 1	6
Passage 2	14
Passage 3	22
Passage 4	30
Passage 5	38
Passage 6	46
Passage 7	54
Passage 8	62
Passage 9	70
Passage 10	77
Passage 11	85
Passage 12	93
Passage 13	101
Passage 14	109
Passage 15	117
Answer Key	**125**
Passage 1	125
Passage 2	125
Passage 3	125
Passage 4	126
Passage 5	126
Passage 6	126
Passage 7	127
Passage 8	127
Passage 9	127
Passage 10	128
Passage 11	128
Passage 12	128
Passage 13	129
Passage 14	129
Passage 15	129

INTRODUCTION
For Parents, Teachers, and Tutors

Developing Writing Skills

In 2017, the state of Virginia adopted new *Standards of Learning*. The *Standards of Learning* describe what students are expected to know. All the exercises and questions in this book cover the *Standards of Learning* introduced in 2017.

Revising and Editing Practice

Each practice set in this book provides practice with both revising and editing tasks. Revising questions involve making changes to strengthen writing. This involve tasks like adding sentences, combining sentences, simplifying sentences, making stronger word choices, removing irrelevant information, and using effective transition words and phrases. Editing tasks involve making changes to correct errors. These errors cover grammar, word usage, capitalization, punctuation, spelling, sentence structure, and paragraphing.

Completing the Practice Sets

Each practice set in this book contains an example of student writing that contains errors or opportunities for improvement. Each passage is followed by 18 multiple-choice questions that ask students to identify and correct an error, or choose the best way to improve the passage.

Student work can be checked after each practice set to determine progress and provide feedback. In this way, students can develop and improve their skills as they complete the sets.

Preparing for the SOL Writing Test

Students are assessed for writing in grade 5. The SOL Writing tests include a writing task and revising and editing tasks. The revising and editing tasks require students to read an example of student writing and answer multiple-choice questions about how to improve or correct the writing. The revising and editing practice sets in this book will prepare students for these tasks.

The SOL Writing tests also include a writing task where students write an essay or narrative. These tasks are scored for overall writing ability. The features expected of strong student writing include remaining focused, having an effective structure, expressing ideas clearly, using effective transitions, using language effectively, and using specific word choices. These tasks are also scored for usage and mechanics, which includes forming sentences correctly, using correct grammar, and having correct spelling, capitalization, and punctuation. The revising and editing tasks in this book will help develop strong writing skills and will improve student performance on these tasks.

Revising and Editing

Practice Sets

Instructions for Students

Read each passage. Each passage contains errors or opportunities for improvement. The questions following each passage will ask you how to correct an error or how to improve the passage.

The sentences in the passage are numbered. Each question will give the sentence number or the paragraph number the question is about. You can reread the sentence to help you answer the question, and some questions may require you to reread a paragraph to answer the question. You can look back at the passage as often as you like.

For each multiple-choice question, read the question carefully. Then select the best answer. Fill in the circle for the correct answer.

Passage 1

Suzanna wrote a short story about a girl who visited a new planet. Read the story and look for any changes that should be made. Then answer the questions that follow.

Planet X

(1) Maria went into space with her Uncle Tom. (2) Uncle Tom made a rocket that could travel through space past pluto. (3) Maria asked her Uncle Tom if she could see a new planet that nobody ever saw before. (4) Uncle Tom said they needed to make her a space suit to keep her safe during the long journey.

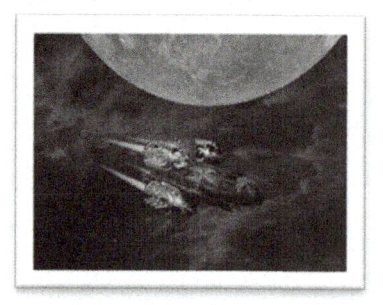

(5) Maria started to make a suit with cereal boxes and plastic water bottles. (6) Uncle Tom said they needed more things. (7) Maria and Uncle Tom made the suit together with pipes aluminum plastic bottles and glass. (8) When they were ready to leave Maria's mother told them to be careful.

(9) The rocket was super fast. (10) Maria took pictures from the rockets small window. (11) They saw rocks floating in space, shooting stars, and even a pear of old sneakers. (12) Maria start to get scared when they got close to Planet X. (13) Uncle Tom told her not to be scared. (14) Maria was very brave and sat in her seat with her seatbelt on tightly. (15) Uncle Tom slowly carefully landed the rocket on Planet X. (16) They quickly got dressed in their space suits with oxygen tanks and left the rocket.

(17) Maria and Uncle Tom were very surprised to be greeted by humans! (18) Maria and Uncle Tom made friends with the people on Planet X. (19) They met the President of Planet X. (20) The President told them that they had never had any visitors from another planet before. (21) Maria took pictures of the strange planet with the President's daughter, Xenaj. (22) Xenaj and Maria quick became good friends. (23) Maria and Xenaj swam underwater with new and interesting creatures that Maria could never have imajined. (24) They saw orange and purple fish that had three heads and seventeen fins. (25) Uncle Tom sent a signal from Planet X to Earth to tell Maria's mother they were enjoying their time on Planet X.

(26) After a month on Planet X, Uncle Tom told Maria they had to go home. (27) Maria's heart sank when she heard the news. (28) She did not want to leave Xenaj, but they took pictures together and promised to send space letters. (29) When Maria and Uncle Tom got home, hundreds of news reporters were camped out all around there house. (30) Maria and Uncle Tom were suddenly famous for their discovery. (31) They gave interviews to magazines and appeared on loads of talk shows.

(32) Even though she was glad to be home, Maria was sad and she missed her friend Xenaj. (33) Then Maria got a space letter from Xenaj. (34) Xenaj invited Maria and her Uncle Tom to come again to Planet X. (35) "Can we go again?" Maria asked. (36) She was thrilled when her uncle said yes.

1 Which word in sentence 2 should be capitalized?

- Ⓐ rocket
- Ⓑ travel
- Ⓒ space
- Ⓓ pluto

2 At the end of sentence 3, the words "ever saw before" are not the right words to use. Which of these shows how to rewrite the sentence?

- Ⓐ Maria asked her Uncle Tom if she could see a new planet that nobody ever seen before.
- Ⓑ Maria asked her Uncle Tom if she could see a new planet that nobody never seen before.
- Ⓒ Maria asked her Uncle Tom if she could see a new planet that nobody had ever seen before.
- Ⓓ Maria asked her Uncle Tom if she could see a new planet that nobody have ever seen before.

3 Which of these shows where commas should be placed in sentence 7?

- Ⓐ Maria and Uncle Tom made the suit together with pipes, aluminum, plastic bottles, and glass.
- Ⓑ Maria and Uncle Tom made the suit together with pipes, aluminum, plastic bottles, and, glass.
- Ⓒ Maria and Uncle Tom made the suit together with, pipes, aluminum, plastic bottles, and glass.
- Ⓓ Maria and Uncle Tom made the suit together, with pipes, aluminum, plastic bottles, and glass.

4 Which of these shows where a comma should be placed in sentence 8?

- Ⓐ When they were ready, to leave Maria's mother told them to be careful.
- Ⓑ When they were ready to leave, Maria's mother told them to be careful.
- Ⓒ When they were ready to leave Maria's mother, told them to be careful.
- Ⓓ When they were ready to leave Maria's mother told them, to be careful.

5 In sentence 9, which phrase would be best to use in place of "super fast"?

- Ⓐ amazingly speedy
- Ⓑ wild and crazy
- Ⓒ just marvelous
- Ⓓ very terrifying

6 Which of these shows how apostrophes should be used in sentence 10?

- Ⓐ Maria took picture's from the rockets small window.
- Ⓑ Maria took pictures from the rocket's small window.
- Ⓒ Maria took picture's from the rocket's small window.
- Ⓓ Maria' took picture's from the rocket's small window.

7 Which change should be made in sentence 11?

- Ⓐ Replace *saw* with *soar*
- Ⓑ Replace *rocks* with *rock's*
- Ⓒ Replace *pear* with *pair*
- Ⓓ Replace *old* with *olden*

8 Sentence 12 does not use the correct verb tense. Which of these shows the correct way to write sentence 12?

- Ⓐ Maria start to got scared when they got close to Planet X.
- Ⓑ Maria started to get scared when they got close to Planet X.
- Ⓒ Maria started to got scared when they got close to Planet X.
- Ⓓ Maria starts to get scared when they got close to Planet X.

9 Which of these shows the correct word to add after *slowly* in sentence 15?

- Ⓐ Uncle Tom slowly or carefully landed the rocket on Planet X.
- Ⓑ Uncle Tom slowly and carefully landed the rocket on Planet X.
- Ⓒ Uncle Tom slowly more carefully landed the rocket on Planet X.
- Ⓓ Uncle Tom slowly then carefully landed the rocket on Planet X.

10 In sentence 17, Suzanna wants to replace "very surprised" with a word that emphasizes how surprised Maria and Uncle Tom were. Which word would Suzanna be best to use?

- Ⓐ amazed
- Ⓑ alarmed
- Ⓒ thrilled
- Ⓓ thankful

11 In sentence 20, which word should replaced *telled*?

- Ⓐ tell
- Ⓑ tells
- Ⓒ told
- Ⓓ tolded

12 In sentence 22, which word should replace *quick*?

- Ⓐ quicker
- Ⓑ quicken
- Ⓒ quickly
- Ⓓ quickness

13   Which change should be made in sentence 23?

  Ⓐ   Replace *swam* with *swimming*

  Ⓑ   Replace *new* with *knew*

  Ⓒ   Replace *creatures* with *creetures*

  Ⓓ   Replace *imajined* with *imagined*

14   In sentence 27, what does the phrase "Maria's heart sank" show?

  Ⓐ   She felt sad.

  Ⓑ   She felt jealous.

  Ⓒ   She felt sick.

  Ⓓ   She felt confused.

15   At the end of sentence 29, which word should replace *there*?

  Ⓐ   they

  Ⓑ   their

  Ⓒ   them

  Ⓓ   they're

16 In sentence 31, Suzanna wants to replace the phrase "loads of" with a phrase that is more formal. Which phrase is the most formal and would be the best replacement?

- Ⓐ heaps of
- Ⓑ lots of
- Ⓒ oodles of
- Ⓓ stacks of

17 In sentence 32, the word *and* is not the best word to use. Which of these shows the best word to use?

- Ⓐ Even though she was glad to be home, Maria was sad after she missed her friend Xenaj.
- Ⓑ Even though she was glad to be home, Maria was sad although she missed her friend Xenaj.
- Ⓒ Even though she was glad to be home, Maria was sad then she missed her friend Xenaj.
- Ⓓ Even though she was glad to be home, Maria was sad because she missed her friend Xenaj.

18 In sentence 35, Suzanna wants to replace *asked* with a word that shows that Maria really wanted her uncle to agree. Which word would be best to use?

- Ⓐ inquired
- Ⓑ pleaded
- Ⓒ said
- Ⓓ shouted

END OF PRACTICE SET

Passage 2

Tricia's class is learning about how to be responsible. Her teacher asked the class to write an essay on what responsibility means to them and how they can demonstrate this skill. Tricia wrote the essay that follows. Read the essay and look for any changes that should be made. Then answer the questions that follow.

Responsibility

(1) To me, responsibility means being able to take care of yourself and make good choses. (2) Responsibility is a skill we work on our whole lives. (3) There are many ways to demonstrate responsibility in school at home and in our social lives. (4) As we grow older, we grow more and more responsible so that one day we may take care of ourself and others successfully.

(5) In school, we are given many assignments and homework that we became responsible for. (6) One way to practice responsibility is by making sure all of this work gets completed on time and to the best of our abillity. (7) My dad teached me how to set aside time to do homework every day. (8) After school, I eat a snack and get to watch a show for half an hour. (9) After that, I know it is time to complete any homework I have. (10) I practice this routine so I dont forget to eat, relax, and finish homework. (11) This helps me become more responsible in school as well. (12) I know that when my teacher gives us a worksheet, I am supposed to use my best effort to finish it and not get off task.

(13) At home, my parents give me chores to finish each week. (14) Every Wednesday I make sure my clothes are put in the hamper and my room is cleaned. (15) This helps me become more responsible for my surroundings. (16) I also make sure to tell my mom or dad when I am going to visit my neighbors so they always no where I am.

(17) Finally, I do my best to take care of my little brother Jasper when I can. (18) My brother is four years old and needs help doing lot of thing. (19) Sometimes I help Jasper get ready for bed and read to he. (20) I know my parents like that I am responsible at home because this helps everything run smoothly in our house.

(21) With friends, I know that I need to make responsible decisions. (22) I learned in school that I should not be swayed by peer pressure. (23) If my friends make a bad choice I know it is my responsibility to say no. (24) It is also my responsibility to be kind and understanding. (25) If my friend is having a bad day, I will ask what is wrong and listen careful to any worries. (26) It is my responsibility as a friend to be there for my own friends.

(27) We can practice responsibility in many ways. (28) It may be hard to make the responsible decision at times. (29) We will get better at this as we grow up. (30) Responsibility is an important skill to learn, practice, and keep in our daily lives. (31) It means you are being good to the people around you, and good to you as well.

1 In sentence 1, what is the correct word to end the sentence?

Ⓐ choose

Ⓑ chooses

Ⓒ choice

Ⓓ choices

2 Which of these shows where commas should be placed in sentence 3?

Ⓐ There are many ways to demonstrate responsibility in school at home, and in our social lives.

Ⓑ There are many ways to demonstrate responsibility, in school at home and in our social lives.

Ⓒ There are many ways to demonstrate responsibility in school, at home, and in our social lives.

Ⓓ There are many ways to demonstrate responsibility in school, at home, and in our, social lives.

3 Which change should be made in sentence 4?

Ⓐ Replace *one* with *won*

Ⓑ Replace *ourself* with *ourselves*

Ⓒ Replace *others* with *other's*

Ⓓ Replace *successfully* with *successful*

4 Which change should be made in sentence 5?

- Ⓐ Replace *are* with *is*
- Ⓑ Replace *given* with *gave*
- Ⓒ Replace *that* with *which*
- Ⓓ Replace *became* with *become*

5 In sentence 6, what is the correct way to spell *abillity*?

- Ⓐ ability
- Ⓑ abilety
- Ⓒ abillety
- Ⓓ abbility

6 In sentence 7, which word should replace *teached*?

- Ⓐ teach
- Ⓑ teaches
- Ⓒ taught
- Ⓓ teaching

7 In sentence 10, which word with an apostrophe should replace *dont*?

- Ⓐ do'nt
- Ⓑ don't
- Ⓒ did'nt
- Ⓓ didn't

8 Tricia wants to rewrite sentence 13 using the word *weekly* instead of "each week." Which sentence shows the best placement of *weekly*?

- Ⓐ At home, weekly my parents give me chores to finish.
- Ⓑ At home, my parents weekly give me chores to finish.
- Ⓒ At home, my parents give me weekly chores to finish.
- Ⓓ At home, my parents give me chores weekly to finish.

9 In sentence 16, the words *no* and *where* are both homophones. Which sentence uses the correct form of both homophones?

- Ⓐ I also make sure to tell my mom or dad when I am going to visit my neighbors so they always no we're I am.
- Ⓑ I also make sure to tell my mom or dad when I am going to visit my neighbors so they always no wear I am.
- Ⓒ I also make sure to tell my mom or dad when I am going to visit my neighbors so they always know where I am.
- Ⓓ I also make sure to tell my mom or dad when I am going to visit my neighbors so they always know we're I am.

10 In sentence 18, Tricia has made an error using the phrase "lot of thing." Which of these shows the correct phrase to use?

- Ⓐ My brother is four years old and needs help doing lots of thing.
- Ⓑ My brother is four years old and needs help doing lot of things.
- Ⓒ My brother is four years old and needs help doing lots of things.
- Ⓓ My brother is four years old and needs help doing lot of thing's.

11 At the end of sentence 19, which word should replace *he*?

- Ⓐ it
- Ⓑ him
- Ⓒ his
- Ⓓ them

12 In sentence 21, which word could be added before *friends*?

- Ⓐ my
- Ⓑ our
- Ⓒ your
- Ⓓ their

13 In sentence 22, what does the word *swayed* mean?

- Ⓐ annoyed
- Ⓑ influenced
- Ⓒ interested
- Ⓓ noticed

14 Which of these shows where a comma should be placed in sentence 23?

- Ⓐ If my friends, make a bad choice I know it is my responsibility to say no.
- Ⓑ If my friends make a bad choice, I know it is my responsibility to say no.
- Ⓒ If my friends make a bad choice I know, it is my responsibility to say no.
- Ⓓ If my friends make a bad choice I know it is my responsibility, to say no.

15 As it is used in sentence 24, which of these means the opposite of *kind*?

- Ⓐ caring
- Ⓑ mean
- Ⓒ selfish
- Ⓓ type

16 Which change should be made in sentence 25?

- Ⓐ Replace *having* with *haveing*
- Ⓑ Replace *wrong* with *rong*
- Ⓒ Replace *listen* with *lissen*
- Ⓓ Replace *careful* with *carefully*

17 Which of these shows the best way to combine sentences 28 and 29?

- Ⓐ It may be hard to make the responsible decision at times, so we will get better at this as we grow up.
- Ⓑ It may be hard to make the responsible decision at times, and we will get better at this as we grow up.
- Ⓒ It may be hard to make the responsible decision at times, but we will get better at this as we grow up.
- Ⓓ It may be hard to make the responsible decision at times, or we will get better at this as we grow up.

18 At the end of sentence 31, *you* is not the right word to use. Which of these shows the right word to use?

- Ⓐ It means you are being good to the people around you, and good to me as well.
- Ⓑ It means you are being good to the people around you, and good to us as well.
- Ⓒ It means you are being good to the people around you, and good to myself as well.
- Ⓓ It means you are being good to the people around you, and good to yourself as well.

END OF PRACTICE SET

Passage 3

George's teacher told the class to write a personal narrative about a day when they learned something new. George wrote about his day at work with his father. Read the personal narrative and look for any changes that should be made. Then answer the questions that follow.

My Day as a Mason

(1) One monday in the summer, my father told me that I was going to work with him. (2) I was surprised because my dad don't have a typical office job with a "bring your kids to work day." (3) My dad is a mason. (4) He lays bricks and makes foundations and stone walls. (5) He works with cement, brick, stone, and his hands all day. (6) I was nervous to go at first, but I was more excited to be spending the day as my dads helper.

(7) We left the house around six o'clock in the morning! (8) I was very tired but my dad made me hot chocolate and we were out the door. (9) The first place we went was someone's house in the town over. (10) My dad and his work partners was building a chimney outside on the patio. (11) My dad got right to work and showed me how to mix the cement and lay it down with a spade. (12) I learned how to place the bricks perfectly so they would be in the right position when the cement dryed. (13) It was so cool to see the chimney take shape.

(14) Next, we went to a neighbor's house to lay a patio foundation. (15) We had to be on time so we could meet the cement truck. (16) The cement truck was humongous. (17) There is a big part of the truck called the mixing drum. (18) The mixing drum is a big steel oval that turns around to kept the cement mixed up. (19) My dad directed the truck to the back of the house. (20) The truck drove over the lawn and left big tracks. (21) Then, the whole mixing drum moved down towards the ground and the cement came out of something called a chute. (22) My dad and his partners had to rake the cement and make sure it was even.

(23) When they finished we got to have lunch outside. (24) My dad packed us sandwiches. (25) I had peanut butter and jelly. (26) My dad had ham and cheese. (27) We sat on empty buckets and told storys and laughed a lot.

(28) After lunch, my dad and I gone back to the first house and continued working on the chimney. (29) We worked until the sun started going down. (30) When it was time to stop, we covered our work with a tarp and held it down with bricks. (31) It's important to keep everything covered in case it rains, my dad explained.

(32) I learned so much from my dad that day. (33) I learned all about what he does at work. (34) I saw how hard he works and how long his days are. (35) I am so happy I got to spend the day with him and be a mason for a day.

Stonemasons use they're skills for laying stones or bricks to make a range of features.

1   Which word in sentence 1 should start with a capital?

   Ⓐ   monday
   Ⓑ   summer
   Ⓒ   told
   Ⓓ   work

2   In sentence 2, which word should replace *don't*?

   Ⓐ   didn't
   Ⓑ   doesn't
   Ⓒ   won't
   Ⓓ   wouldn't

3   Which change should be made in sentence 6?

   Ⓐ   Replace *nervous* with *nervice*
   Ⓑ   Replace *but* with *so*
   Ⓒ   Replace *excited* with *excitted*
   Ⓓ   Replace *dads* with *dad's*

4 George wants to rewrite sentence 8 as two sentences. Which of these shows the best way to write two sentences?

- Ⓐ I was very tired, but my dad. He made me hot chocolate and we were out the door.
- Ⓑ I was very tired. Also, my dad made me hot chocolate and we were out the door.
- Ⓒ I was very tired, so my dad made me hot chocolate. Then we were out the door.
- Ⓓ I was very tired and my dad made me hot chocolate. After, we were out the door.

5 In sentence 10, which word should replace *was*?

- Ⓐ is
- Ⓑ are
- Ⓒ were
- Ⓓ been

6 Which change should be made in sentence 12?

- Ⓐ Replace *place* with *placed*
- Ⓑ Replace *perfectly* with *perfect*
- Ⓒ Replace *right* with *write*
- Ⓓ Replace *dryed* with *dried*

7 In sentence 13, George wants to replace the phrase "so cool" with a word with the same meaning. Which would should George use?

- Ⓐ amazing
- Ⓑ chilly
- Ⓒ surprising
- Ⓓ modern

8 Which sentence in paragraph 3 would be best to end with an exclamation point?

- Ⓐ Sentence 15
- Ⓑ Sentence 16
- Ⓒ Sentence 17
- Ⓓ Sentence 18

9 In sentence 18, which word should replace *kept*?

- Ⓐ keep
- Ⓑ keeps
- Ⓒ keeper
- Ⓓ keeping

10 Which of these shows where a comma should be placed in sentence 23?

- Ⓐ When they finished, we got to have lunch outside.
- Ⓑ When they finished we got, to have lunch outside.
- Ⓒ When they finished we got to have, lunch outside.
- Ⓓ When they finished we got to have lunch, outside.

11 George wants to combine sentences 25 and 26. Which of these is the best way to combine the two sentences?

- Ⓐ I had peanut butter and jelly, then my dad had ham and cheese.
- Ⓑ I had peanut butter and jelly, while my dad had ham and cheese.
- Ⓒ I had peanut butter and jelly, anyway my dad had ham and cheese.
- Ⓓ I had peanut butter and jelly, although my dad had ham and cheese.

12 In sentence 27, which of these should replace *storys*?

- Ⓐ story's
- Ⓑ storrys
- Ⓒ stories
- Ⓓ storries

13 In sentence 28, which word should replace *gone*?

- Ⓐ go
- Ⓑ got
- Ⓒ went
- Ⓓ were

14 Sentence 29 can be rewritten to express the ideas in a simpler way. Which of these shows the correct way to rewrite the sentence?

- Ⓐ We worked until noon.
- Ⓑ We worked until dawn.
- Ⓒ We worked until sunrise.
- Ⓓ We worked until sunset.

15 Which of these shows the correct placement of quotation marks in sentence 31?

- Ⓐ "It's important to keep everything covered in case it rains, my dad explained."
- Ⓑ "It's important to keep everything covered in case it rains," my dad explained.
- Ⓒ "It's important to keep everything covered in case it rains", my dad explained.
- Ⓓ "It's important to keep everything covered in case it rains," my dad explained."

16 In sentence 35, which two words could be shortened into one word by using an apostrophe?

- Ⓐ I am
- Ⓑ got to
- Ⓒ with him
- Ⓓ a day

17 George wants to add the sentence below to the last paragraph.

Now I understand why he is so tired in the evenings!

Which of these would be the best place for the sentence?

- Ⓐ After sentence 32
- Ⓑ After sentence 33
- Ⓒ After sentence 34
- Ⓓ After sentence 35

18 Which change should be made in the caption at the end of the passage?

- Ⓐ Replace *they're* with *their*
- Ⓑ Add a comma after *stones*
- Ⓒ Replace *make* with *made*
- Ⓓ Replace *features* with *feetures*

END OF PRACTICE SET

Passage 4

Luke's teacher asked him to write an essay on an important person in his life. Luke wrote an essay about his grandmother. Read the essay and look for any changes that should be made. Then answer the questions that follow.

My Grandma

(1) My grandma is a very important person in my life. (2) She has always cared for and suported me. (3) I know my grandma always wants the best for me. (4) She is always kind understanding and thoughtful. (5) I am very lucky to have my grandma in my life.

(6) My grandma teaches me things all the time. (7) She helps me with homework when I need it. (8) Last year, I have to give a report on my family tree. (9) My grandma went through old photos with me for my poster. (10) She told me all about my ancestors and what her life was like as a child.

(11) I learned that my grandma grew up in new york city. (12) She worked as a waitress when she was in high school and learned how to cook from the chef. (13) After high school, she went to culinary school to learn to be a chef. (14) When my grandma graduated from college, she worked hard and eventually opened her own greek restaurant. (15) She closed her restaurant and retired after I was born. (16) She still makes really tasty food for our family.

(17) My grandma is always their when I need her. (18) She was at the hospital when I was born and was my first babysitter. (19) Whenever my parents needed to leave the house my grandma came over to watch me. (20) I will always remember how much I loved listening to my grandma read to me. (21) My grandma read me nursery rhymes and would act out the stories so I would understate them better.

(22) When I started playing baseball, my grandma gave me my dad's old mitt. (23) My coach has really helped me improve my batting. (24) Grandma was at every game cheering me on. (25) The team loved it when my grandma would bring orange slices to eats. (26) I hit my first home run when my grandma was watching me play. (27) After the game, she took me out for ice cream to celebration.

(28) On my last birthday, my grandma took me to an amusement park. (29) She went on every ride with me. (30) She was 70 years old. (31) That was one of the best days I had all year.

(32) My grandma will always be one of my bestest friends. (33) I love spending time with her. (34) Wether we are cooking, reading, or just running errands, I always have a wonderful time.

1 In sentence 2, what is the correct way to spell *suported*?

- Ⓐ saported
- Ⓑ sapported
- Ⓒ supported
- Ⓓ suportted

2 Which of these shows the correct way to place commas in sentence 4?

- Ⓐ She is always, kind understanding and, thoughtful.
- Ⓑ She is always kind, understanding, and thoughtful.
- Ⓒ She is always kind, understanding, and, thoughtful.
- Ⓓ She is always, kind, understanding, and, thoughtful.

3 Sentence 8 does not use the correct verb tense. What is the correct way to write sentence 8?

- Ⓐ Last year, I had to give a report on my family tree.
- Ⓑ Last year, I had to given a report on my family tree.
- Ⓒ Last year, I have to given a report on my family tree.
- Ⓓ Last year, I having to give a report on my family tree.

4 Luke wants to shorten sentence 10. Which of these shows a correct way he could shorten the sentence?

- Ⓐ She told me all about my ancestors and her child.
- Ⓑ She told me all about my ancestors and her children.
- Ⓒ She told me all about my ancestors and her childish.
- Ⓓ She told me all about my ancestors and her childhood.

5 In sentence 11, how should "new york city" be capitalized?

- Ⓐ New york city
- Ⓑ New York city
- Ⓒ new York city
- Ⓓ New York City

6 Which word in sentence 14 should be capitalized?

- Ⓐ college
- Ⓑ hard
- Ⓒ greek
- Ⓓ restaurant

7 In sentence 16, Luke wants to replace the phrase "really tasty" with a word with the same meaning. Which word would Luke be best to use?

Ⓐ surprising

Ⓑ costly

Ⓒ creative

Ⓓ delicious

8 Which change should be made in sentence 17?

Ⓐ Replace *is* with *are*

Ⓑ Replace *always* with *anyway*

Ⓒ Replace *their* with *there*

Ⓓ Replace *her* with *it*

9 Which of these shows where a comma should be placed in sentence 19?

Ⓐ Whenever my parents, needed to leave the house my grandma came over to watch me.

Ⓑ Whenever my parents needed to leave, the house my grandma came over to watch me.

Ⓒ Whenever my parents needed to leave the house, my grandma came over to watch me.

Ⓓ Whenever my parents needed to leave the house my grandma, came over to watch me.

10 In sentence 21, *understate* is not the correct word. Which word should be used in place of *understate*?

- Ⓐ understand
- Ⓑ underneath
- Ⓒ undertook
- Ⓓ underuse

11 Luke wants to add a topic sentence to introduce the ideas in paragraph 5. Which sentence would Luke be best to add before sentence 22?

- Ⓐ Grandma has more energy than anyone I know.
- Ⓑ Grandma supports me in everything that I do.
- Ⓒ Grandma is always a lot of fun to be with.
- Ⓓ Grandma never seems to stop thinking about food.

12 In sentence 25, which word should replace *eats*?

- Ⓐ ate
- Ⓑ eat
- Ⓒ eaten
- Ⓓ eating

13 Which sentence does NOT belong in paragraph 5?
- Ⓐ Sentence 22
- Ⓑ Sentence 23
- Ⓒ Sentence 24
- Ⓓ Sentence 25

14 In sentence 27, which of these shows the correct word to replace *celebration* with?
- Ⓐ After the game, she took me out for ice cream to celebrate.
- Ⓑ After the game, she took me out for ice cream to celebrates.
- Ⓒ After the game, she took me out for ice cream to celebrated.
- Ⓓ After the game, she took me out for ice cream to celebrating.

15 Which of these shows the best way to combine sentences 29 and 30?
- Ⓐ She went on every ride with me, after all she was 70 years old.
- Ⓑ She went on every ride with me, even though she was 70 years old.
- Ⓒ She went on every ride with me, in case she was 70 years old.
- Ⓓ She went on every ride with me, for example she was 70 years old.

16 Sentence 31 can be rewritten to express the ideas in a simpler way. Which of these shows the correct way to rewrite the sentence?

- Ⓐ It was the highroad of my year.
- Ⓑ It was the highland of my year.
- Ⓒ It was the highflyer of my year.
- Ⓓ It was the highlight of my year.

17 Which change should be made in sentence 32?

- Ⓐ Replace *will* with *would*
- Ⓑ Replace *one* with *won*
- Ⓒ Replace *bestest* with *best*
- Ⓓ Replace *friends* with *friend's*

18 Which word in sentence 34 is spelled incorrectly?

- Ⓐ wether
- Ⓑ reading
- Ⓒ errands
- Ⓓ wonderful

END OF PRACTICE SET

Passage 5

Ella's teacher asked her to write a report on the California Gold Rush. Read the report and look for any changes that should be made. Then answer the questions that follow.

The Gold Rush

(1) The California Gold Rush started in the Year 1848 when James Sutter discovered gold in Coloma, which is an area about 30 miles inland from Sacramento. (2) Marshall was the first to find small pieces of gold when he was building a sawmill for his boss John Sutter. (3) Marshall and Sutter tried to keep this discovery a secret. (4) Unfortunately, the story got out and soon newspapers were reporting on the gold. (5) Marshalls discovery became national news. (6) People all around the world decided to make the move to California.

(7) To get to California, people traveled by wagons and boats. (8) People who traveled by covered wagon had to cross deserts and clime mountains. (9) They put up with high temperatures in the deserts and freezing temperatures in the mountains. (10) Many travelers died during this journey that was dangerous. (11) Travelers who went by boat had to deal with storms and disease. (12) There was no easy way to get to California.

(13) Close to 90,000 people rushed to California in 1849. (14) These people became known as the "forty-niners." (15) Forty-niners usually learned how to mine on the job. (16) To mine for gold, miners needed various supplies. (17) Mining required mining pans shovels and a pick. (18) People who sold supplies made a lot of money, and usually made more then the miners.

(19) People who came to California was hoping to get rich from this gold. (20) So many people came at once and the riverbanks became crowded. (21) By 1850, gold was very hard to find. (22) People lost a lot of money and had a hard time affording food and fresh water. (23) Unfortunately, many people died from disease and accidents.

People traveled to California from across America and from all over the world. Everyone was hoping to make it rich, but very few did.

(24) The California Gold Rush ended in 1859 once silver was discovered in Nevada. (25) Many mining towns were deserted. (26) The population rapidly decreased. (27) California though did benefit from the Gold Rush. (28) Many businesses grew and California became prosperous. (29) After the Gold Rush, many towns became "ghost towns." (30) The town of Bodie in California became a ghost town and is now a populer tourist attraction.

(31) There have been many other gold rush. (32) In the United States, Colorado and Alaska were sights of gold rushes in the past. (33) The California Gold Rush, however, is the most well-known and successful gold rush in history.

1 Which word in sentence 1 should NOT be capitalized?
- Ⓐ Year
- Ⓑ James
- Ⓒ Coloma
- Ⓓ Sacramento

2 Which of these shows where a comma should be placed in sentence 2?
- Ⓐ Marshall was the first to find small pieces of gold, when he was building a sawmill for his boss John Sutter.
- Ⓑ Marshall was the first to find small pieces of gold when he was building, a sawmill for his boss John Sutter.
- Ⓒ Marshall was the first to find small pieces of gold when he was building a sawmill, for his boss John Sutter.
- Ⓓ Marshall was the first to find small pieces of gold when he was building a sawmill for his boss, John Sutter.

3 Which change should be made in sentence 5?
- Ⓐ Replace *Marshalls* with *Marshall's*
- Ⓑ Replace *discovery* with *discovering*
- Ⓒ Replace *became* with *become*
- Ⓓ Replace *news* with *new's*

4 In sentence 6, Ella wants to add a transition phrase to better link the ideas in sentences 5 and 6. Which transition phrase would Ella be best to use?

Ⓐ Then again, people all around the world decided to make the move to California.

Ⓑ For example, people all around the world decided to make the move to California.

Ⓒ In contrast, people all around the world decided to make the move to California.

Ⓓ As a result, people all around the world decided to make the move to California.

5 Which word in sentence 8 is spelled incorrectly?

Ⓐ covered

Ⓑ wagon

Ⓒ deserts

Ⓓ clime

6 Which of these shows the best way to rewrite sentence 10?

Ⓐ Many dangerous travelers died during this journey.

Ⓑ Many travelers died, dangerous during this journey.

Ⓒ Many travelers died during this dangerous journey.

Ⓓ Many travelers died during this journey, dangerous.

7 Which of these shows where commas should be placed in sentence 17?

Ⓐ Mining required mining pans, shovels, and a pick.
Ⓑ Mining required, mining pans, shovels, and a pick.
Ⓒ Mining required mining pans, shovels, and, a pick.
Ⓓ Mining required, mining pans, shovels, and, a pick.

8 Which change should be made in sentence 18?

Ⓐ Replace *who* with *which*
Ⓑ Replace *money* with *moneys*
Ⓒ Replace *usually* with *usual*
Ⓓ Replace *then* with *than*

9 In sentence 19, which word should replace *was*?

Ⓐ are
Ⓑ be
Ⓒ is
Ⓓ were

10 In sentence 20, *and* is not the right word to connect the clauses. Which of these shows the best word to use?

- Ⓐ So many people came at once for the riverbanks became crowded.
- Ⓑ So many people came at once that the riverbanks became crowded.
- Ⓒ So many people came at once then the riverbanks became crowded.
- Ⓓ So many people came at once while the riverbanks became crowded.

11 Ella wants to change sentence 21 to emphasize how hard it was to find gold. Which of these changes makes finding gold seem the hardest?

- Ⓐ By 1850, gold was simple to find.
- Ⓑ By 1850, gold was almost impossible to find.
- Ⓒ By 1850, gold was tricky to find.
- Ⓓ By 1850, gold was somewhat difficult to find.

12 Ella wants to rewrite sentence 22 by replacing the phrase "had a hard time." Which of these shows the correct word to use to describe how people had a difficult time?

- Ⓐ People lost a lot of money and shuffled to afford food and fresh water.
- Ⓑ People lost a lot of money and startled to afford food and fresh water.
- Ⓒ People lost a lot of money and struggled to afford food and fresh water.
- Ⓓ People lost a lot of money and stumbled to afford food and fresh water.

13 In sentence 23, which of these shows a way to replace the transition word *unfortunately* without changing the meaning of the sentence?

   Ⓐ   Certainly, many people died from disease and accidents.

   Ⓑ   Luckily, many people died from disease and accidents.

   Ⓒ   Quickly, many people died from disease and accidents.

   Ⓓ   Sadly, many people died from disease and accidents.

14 Ella wants to combine sentences 25 and 26. Which of these is the best way to combine the sentences?

   Ⓐ   The population rapidly decreased, nor many mining towns were deserted.

   Ⓑ   The population rapidly decreased, yet many mining towns were deserted.

   Ⓒ   The population rapidly decreased, and many mining towns were deserted.

   Ⓓ   The population rapidly decreased, but many mining towns were deserted.

15 Which of these shows where commas should be placed in sentence 27?

   Ⓐ   California, though, did benefit from the Gold Rush.

   Ⓑ   California, though did benefit, from the Gold Rush.

   Ⓒ   California though, did benefit, from the Gold Rush.

   Ⓓ   California though did benefit, from the, Gold Rush.

16 In sentence 30, what is the correct way to spell *populer*?

- Ⓐ popüller
- Ⓑ popular
- Ⓒ poppular
- Ⓓ poppuler

17 Which change should be made in sentence 31?

- Ⓐ Replace *There* with *Their*
- Ⓑ Replace *been* with *be*
- Ⓒ Replace *other* with *another*
- Ⓓ Replace *rush* with *rushes*

18 Which change should be made in sentence 32?

- Ⓐ Remove the comma after *States*
- Ⓑ Change *Colorado* and *Alaska* to lower case
- Ⓒ Replace *sights* with *sites*
- Ⓓ Replace *past* with *passed*

END OF PRACTICE SET

Passage 6

The teacher asked Ethan and his classmates to write about a country that they would like to visit. Ethan chose the United Arab Emirates as the country he would like to visit. Read the essay and look for any changes that should be made. Then answer the questions that follow.

The Seven Emirates

(1) My dad grew up in the United Arab Emirates but he wanted to study abroad, so he decide to move to Arizona. (2) He met my mom while in Arizona and decided to stay permanently. (3) I was born after they got married. (4) The United States is the only country I have been too.

(5) Dad likes to tell me about the UAE. (6) He told me that it weren't always as beautiful as it is now. (7) It used to be just full of sand and small buildings. (8) He said that oil was the UAE's key to earning money. (9) He also said that oil would not last. (10) Because of this, they decided to attract tourists. (11) He says it is also a peacefull country. (12) The UAE accepts any foreigner who wants to live there.

(13) UAE has many huge and stunning malls. (14) Dad told me that one mall had a giant aquarium with sharks inside. (15) He told me there were big bikes that you can ride in the deserts. (16) He told me about delightful Arabian food available almost every where. (17) We usually only have tastey Arabian food at home. (18) Dad told me that the UAE has the most tall building in the world, many beautiful buildings, and good roads. (19) He even told me that there is an island shaped like a palm tree's leaves!

The United Arab Emirates is popular with tourists, and offers a wide range of activities. You can go from relaxing on a beach to riding through a desert, and then return for dinner in the city.

(20) My mom and dad are both Muslim. (21) My mom changed her religion so she could be with dad. (22) Was a big decision for her to make. (23) They told me it was a change that was good. (24) My dad sometimes wears his special white outfit on special occasions. (25) He tells me that this is the traditional outfit of Emirati men and is called Kandura. (26) My mom likes to where plain dresses that reach the floor and cover nearly her whole body. (27) She also has a special outfit called Abaya. (28) She wears it during special occasions. (29) They told me that it is a common thing to wear in the UAE.

(30) Someday, I want me family to visit this country. (31) I don't want to live there. (32) All my friends and other family live here so I think I will be lonely there. (33) But I would like to visit to see the beautiful malls, the island shaped like a palm tree's leaves. (34) I also want to visit so I can ride a quad bike through the desert. (35) That would be absolutely amazing. (36) I think that visiting the UAE would be an exciting adventure I would never forget.

1 In sentence 1, which word should replace *decide*?

  Ⓐ decides

  Ⓑ decided

  Ⓒ decider

  Ⓓ deciding

2 Sentence 4 contains the homophones *been* and *too*. Which sentence uses the correct form of both homophones?

  Ⓐ Arizona is the only country I have bean too.

  Ⓑ Arizona is the only country I have bean two.

  Ⓒ Arizona is the only country I have been to.

  Ⓓ Arizona is the only country I have been two.

3 In sentence 6, which word should replace *weren't*?

  Ⓐ wasn't

  Ⓑ won't

  Ⓒ hasn't

  Ⓓ haven't

4 Which of these shows the best way to combine sentences 8 and 9?

- Ⓐ He said that oil was the UAE's key to earning money, so that oil would not last.
- Ⓑ He said that oil was the UAE's key to earning money, but that oil would not last.
- Ⓒ He said that oil was the UAE's key to earning money, then that oil would not last.
- Ⓓ He said that oil was the UAE's key to earning money, now that oil would not last.

5 Which change should be made in sentence 11?

- Ⓐ Replace *says* with *saying*
- Ⓑ Replace *it* with *they*
- Ⓒ Replace *is* with *are*
- Ⓓ Replace *peacefull* with *peaceful*

6 In sentence 12, Ethan wants to replace the word *accepts* with a word that makes the UAE sound friendlier. Which word would Ethan be best to use?

- Ⓐ admits
- Ⓑ allows
- Ⓒ takes
- Ⓓ welcomes

7 Which change should be made in sentence 16?

- Ⓐ Replace *told* with *tell*
- Ⓑ Replace *delightful* with *deliteful*
- Ⓒ Replace *almost* with *all most*
- Ⓓ Replace *every where* with *everywhere*

8 Which word in paragraph 3 is spelled incorrectly?

- Ⓐ *stunning*
- Ⓑ *giant*
- Ⓒ *sharks*
- Ⓓ *tastey*

9 In sentence 18, which word should replace "most tall"?

- Ⓐ tall
- Ⓑ taller
- Ⓒ tallest
- Ⓓ tallness

10 Which sentence in paragraph 4 is NOT a complete sentence?

   Ⓐ   Sentence 20
   Ⓑ   Sentence 21
   Ⓒ   Sentence 22
   Ⓓ   Sentence 23

11 Sentence 23 can be rewritten to express the ideas in a simpler way. Which of these shows how to rewrite the sentence without changing its meaning?

   Ⓐ   They told me it was a costly change.
   Ⓑ   They told me it was a difficult change.
   Ⓒ   They told me it was a positive change.
   Ⓓ   They told me it was a special change.

12 Sentence 26 contains homophones. Which of these describes a change that should be made to correct the wrong use of a homophone?

   Ⓐ   Replace *where* with *wear*
   Ⓑ   Replace *plain* with *plane*
   Ⓒ   Replace *floor* with *flaw*
   Ⓓ   Replace *whole* with *hole*

13 Which of these shows the best way to combine sentences 27 and 28?

- Ⓐ She also has a special outfit called Abaya, wears it during special occasions.
- Ⓑ She also has a special outfit called Abaya, she wears it during special occasions.
- Ⓒ She also has a special outfit called Abaya, and she wears during special occasions.
- Ⓓ She also has a special outfit called Abaya, which she wears during special occasions.

14 As it is used in sentence 29, which word means the opposite of *common*?

- Ⓐ comfortable
- Ⓑ easy
- Ⓒ popular
- Ⓓ rare

15 In sentence 30, which word should replace *me*?

- Ⓐ my
- Ⓑ mine
- Ⓒ us
- Ⓓ we

16 In sentence 32, which word should replace *will*?

- Ⓐ then
- Ⓑ am
- Ⓒ must
- Ⓓ would

17 Which change should be made in sentence 33?

- Ⓐ Replace *like* with *liking*
- Ⓑ Replace *see* with *sea*
- Ⓒ Replace the comma with *and*
- Ⓓ Replace *shaped* with *shapes*

18 Which sentence in the last paragraph would be best to end with an exclamation mark?

- Ⓐ Sentence 30
- Ⓑ Sentence 31
- Ⓒ Sentence 34
- Ⓓ Sentence 35

END OF PRACTICE SET

Passage 7

The teacher asked Leslie and her classmates to write about their favorite book. Leslie could not choose between her favorite books. She wrote about both of them. Read the essay and look for any changes that should be made. Then answer the questions that follow.

My Two Favorite Books

(1) I decided that I could not choose between these two books, I will talk about both of them. (2) In all the years that I has been reading, these two books stick out to me the most. (3) I really love reading and have many favorites, so it was difficult to select just these two.

(4) The first book is called *Stargirl* and it was writed by Jerry Spinelli. (5) The book is narrated by a twelve-year-old named Leo. (6) Leo meets a girl named Susan Caraway, which likes to call herself Stargirl. (7) Stargirl was a very weird girl to Leo and his schoolmates. (8) Stargirl used to be homeschooled and she doesn't really like blendding in with other people. (9) While her schoolmates would wear jeans and t-shirts, she would wear long dresses and large hats. (10) She even has a pet rat that she brings to school with herself each day. (11) Leo likes Stargirl, and befriends her. (12) They soon become great friends. (13) But Stargirl is being shunned by the others, and they start treating Leo the same way. (14) Leo could not handle this and decided to stop being friends with her. (15) In the end, Stargirl decided to move away.

(16) *Someday Angeline* is a book by Louis Sachar. (17) It is about an eight-year-old girl who was so intelligent that she got sent to sixth grade. (18) Her widowed father worked hard so that Angeline may get a good future. (19) Angeline is always picked on by her sixth grade classmates. (20) Her teacher thinks poor of her because she is too young. (21) Her only friends are the fifth grade teacher, Miss Turbone, and Gary Boone, an unpopular fifth grader. (22) Angeline became so unhappy with school that she chose not to go for a weak without her father knowing. (23) She went to the beach one day and nearly drowned, just like her mother did. (24) In the end, Angeline moved down one grade to be with both Gary and Miss Turbone, and now she couldn't be any happy.

(25) These books are similar because they both include someone who doesn't fit in with the people around them. (26) During someone's time as a child, this can have a major effect. (27) Angeline nearly drowned because she don't want to go to school and Stargirl had to move away because no one accepted her. (28) Books like these teach us at a young age that we should always treat people with kind. (29) This is an important mesage that every young person should learn, and remember to apply during life. (30) We all should think of others and take action when we can. (31) You never know how a simple act of kindness could affect someone's life.

These to books will make you think about how you treat others.

1 In sentence 1, which word should be placed after the comma?

- Ⓐ but
- Ⓑ so
- Ⓒ or
- Ⓓ and

2 In sentence 2, "has been" is not the correct verb tense. Which of these shows the sentence with the correct verb tense?

- Ⓐ In all the years that I have been reading, these two books stick out to me most.
- Ⓑ In all the years that I having been reading, these two books stick out to me the most.
- Ⓒ In all the years that I has being reading, these two books stick out to me the most.
- Ⓓ In all the years that I have being reading, these two books stick out to me the most.

3 In sentence 4, which word should replace *writed*?

- Ⓐ write
- Ⓑ wrote
- Ⓒ writing
- Ⓓ written

4 In sentence 6, which word should replace *which*?

- Ⓐ her
- Ⓑ she
- Ⓒ who
- Ⓓ that

5 Which change should be made in sentence 8?

- Ⓐ Replace *be* with *been*
- Ⓑ Replace *she* with *her*
- Ⓒ Replace *doesn't* with *does'nt*
- Ⓓ Replace *blendding* with *blending*

6 Leslie would like to add a phrase to the start of sentence 9 to better connect it with sentence 8. Which of these shows the best phrase to use?

- Ⓐ Of course, while her schoolmates would wear jeans and t-shirts, she would wear long dresses and large hats.
- Ⓑ For example, while her schoolmates would wear jeans and t-shirts, she would wear long dresses and large hats.
- Ⓒ In other words, while her schoolmates would wear jeans and t-shirts, she would wear long dresses and large hats.
- Ⓓ In summary, while her schoolmates would wear jeans and t-shirts, she would wear long dresses and large hats.

7 In sentence 10, which word should replace *herself*?

- Ⓐ it
- Ⓑ her
- Ⓒ she
- Ⓓ them

8 Sentence 18 can be improved by replacing the words "may get". Which of these shows the best words to replace "may get" with?

- Ⓐ Her widowed father worked hard so that Angeline would do a good future.
- Ⓑ Her widowed father worked hard so that Angeline might find a good future.
- Ⓒ Her widowed father worked hard so that Angeline should be a good future.
- Ⓓ Her widowed father worked hard so that Angeline could have a good future.

9 Which change should be made in sentence 20?

- Ⓐ Replace *thinks* with *think's*
- Ⓑ Replace *poor* with *poorly*
- Ⓒ Replace *too* with *two*
- Ⓓ Replace *young* with *youngest*

10 Which change should be made in sentence 22?

　　Ⓐ   Replace *became* with *become*

　　Ⓑ   Replace *chose* with *choose*

　　Ⓒ   Replace *weak* with *week*

　　Ⓓ   Replace *knowing* with *nowing*

11 In sentence 24, which word should replace *happy*?

　　Ⓐ   happiness

　　Ⓑ   happier

　　Ⓒ   happening

　　Ⓓ   happiest

12 Sentence 26 can be written more simply. Which of these shows the best way to write the sentence?

　　Ⓐ   During someone's childish, this can have a major effect.

　　Ⓑ   During someone's children, this can have a major effect.

　　Ⓒ   During someone's childhood, this can have a major effect.

　　Ⓓ   During someone's child, this can have a major effect.

13 In sentence 27, which word should replace *don't*?

- Ⓐ wasn't
- Ⓑ can't
- Ⓒ couldn't
- Ⓓ didn't

14 In sentence 28, which word should replace *kind*?

- Ⓐ kinder
- Ⓑ kindest
- Ⓒ kindly
- Ⓓ kindness

15 Which word in sentence 29 is spelled incorrectly?

- Ⓐ important
- Ⓑ mesage
- Ⓒ apply
- Ⓓ during

16 In sentence 30, Leslie wants to replace *should* with a word that makes it seem more important that people think of others. Which of these shows the best word to use?

    Ⓐ   We all may think of others and take action when we can.

    Ⓑ   We all can think of others and take action when we can.

    Ⓒ   We all must think of others and take action when we can.

    Ⓓ   We all could think of others and take action when we can.

17 A dictionary entry for the word *simple* is shown below.

> **simple** *adj.* 1. easy to understand 2. easy to do
> 3. plain or not decorated 4. made up of only one part

Which meaning of the word *simple* is used in sentence 31?

    Ⓐ   Meaning 1

    Ⓑ   Meaning 2

    Ⓒ   Meaning 3

    Ⓓ   Meaning 4

18 Which change should be made in the caption at the end of the passage?

    Ⓐ   Replace *to* with *two*

    Ⓑ   Replace *will* with *would*

    Ⓒ   Replace *about* with *around*

    Ⓓ   Replace *others* with *other's*

END OF PRACTICE SET

Passage 8

Julie and her classmates were asked to write about a time they received a gift. Julie decided to write about the time her grandmother knitted her a sweater. Read the personal narrative and look for any changes that should be made. Then answer the questions that follow.

When Gran Knitted Me A Sweater

(1) Christmas Eve was the time when all my Relatives from across the United States came to see us. (2) There were aunts uncles cousins and grandparents. (3) They also brought presents with them, excited me a lot. (4) I watched them place all the presents one by one under the Christmas tree. (5) I hugged all of them and spoke to the relatives who I had not ever got to meet.

(6) My grandma seemed the most hesitant to hug me. (7) She looked at me for the longest time before she reached out to hug me awkward. (8) I didn't know what was wrong. (9) "Does she think I am too skinny or not pretty enough?" I mumbled to myself. (10) It made me feel weird.

(11) I kept noticing that my grandmother looked really unhappy during the party. (12) She did not say a word during dinner and would not tell anyone why she was sad when she was asked. (13) I had no idea why she seemed so unhappy. (14) She didn't seem that way until the moment she looked at me.

(15) When it was finally time to start opening presents, I tore them open one by one to find lovely things. (16) I got clothes, toys, and gadgets that I'd always wanted. (17) I watched as my other cousins opened their gifts and loved them too. (18) I had one gift left and it was a tiny pink parcel.

(19) You wouldn't want that at all, Julie, Grandma told me. (20) It was the first time she had spoke since she arrived.

(21) She tried to take the present away but me mom said I could open it if I wanted to. (22) I told my grandma that I wanted to see it. (23) She gave up and let me have my present. (24) When I opened it, I found the most small sweater I had ever seen. (25) It looked like it was made for a 5-year-old.

(26) "I didn't know how big you've gotten," my grandma said. (27) She seemed so disappointed in herself that I almost cryed.

(28) It's alright, Gran! I told her and gave her a big hug. (29) "You knitted a sweater for my teddy, it will fit him perfectly!" (30) I had an old teddy I never got tired of and I didn't want to disappoint my grandma. (31) My teddy bear been wearing that special sweater ever since, and he is always sitting proudly on my bed. (32) All the time I see him, I think of Grandma and how much she wanted to do something special for me.

1 Which word in the title should NOT be capitalized?

Ⓐ Gran

Ⓑ Knitted

Ⓒ Me

Ⓓ A

2 Which word in sentence 1 should NOT be capitalized?

Ⓐ Eve

Ⓑ Relatives

Ⓒ United

Ⓓ States

3 Which of these shows where commas should be placed in sentence 2?

Ⓐ There were, aunts uncles cousins, and grandparents.

Ⓑ There were aunts, uncles, cousins, and, grandparents.

Ⓒ There were aunts, uncles, cousins, and grandparents.

Ⓓ There were, aunts, uncles, cousins, and grandparents.

4 Sentence 3 needs a word added after the comma to make a complete sentence. Which of these shows the correct word to use?

- Ⓐ They also brought presents with them, that excited me a lot.
- Ⓑ They also brought presents with them, which excited me a lot.
- Ⓒ They also brought presents with them, they excited me a lot.
- Ⓓ They also brought presents with them, much excited me a lot.

5 In sentence 5, which word should replace "not ever"?

- Ⓐ neither
- Ⓑ never
- Ⓒ either
- Ⓓ whether

6 Which change should be made in sentence 7?

- Ⓐ Replace *longest* with *longer*
- Ⓑ Replace *reached* with *reaches*
- Ⓒ Replace *out* with *outer*
- Ⓓ Replace *awkward* with *awkwardly*

7 Julie wants to replace the words "really unhappy" in sentence 11 with a better word. Which word would Julie be best to use?

- Ⓐ content
- Ⓑ dazed
- Ⓒ miserable
- Ⓓ puzzled

8 In sentence 12, the words "would not" can be shortened. Which of these shows how to write "would not" as a contraction?

- Ⓐ would't
- Ⓑ would'nt
- Ⓒ wouldn't
- Ⓓ would'not

9 In sentence 16, what is *I'd* short for?

- Ⓐ I did
- Ⓑ I had
- Ⓒ I would
- Ⓓ I could

10 Which of these shows how quotation marks should be used in sentence 19?

- Ⓐ "You wouldn't want that at all," Julie, Grandma told me.
- Ⓑ "You wouldn't want that at all, Julie," Grandma told me.
- Ⓒ "You wouldn't want that at all, Julie, Grandma" told me.
- Ⓓ "You wouldn't want that at all, Julie, Grandma told me."

11 In sentence 20, which word should replace *spoke*?

- Ⓐ speak
- Ⓑ speaks
- Ⓒ spoken
- Ⓓ spoking

12 In sentence 21, which word should replace *me*?

- Ⓐ I
- Ⓑ she
- Ⓒ my
- Ⓓ mine

13 In sentence 24, Julie wants to replace "most small" with a better word. Which word would Julie be best to use?

- Ⓐ gentler
- Ⓑ tiniest
- Ⓒ smarter
- Ⓓ silliest

14 Which change should be made in sentence 27?

- Ⓐ Replace *disappointed* with *disappointment*
- Ⓑ Replace *herself* with *oneself*
- Ⓒ Replace *that* with *than*
- Ⓓ Replace *cryed* with *cried*

15 Which of these shows the correct way to use punctuation marks in sentence 28?

- Ⓐ "It's alright, Gran"! I told her and gave her a big hug.
- Ⓑ "It's alright, Gran!" I told her and gave her a big hug.
- Ⓒ "It's alright, Gran! I told her" and gave her a big hug.
- Ⓓ "It's alright, Gran! I told her and gave her a big hug."

16 In sentence 29, Julie needs to add a word after the comma to form a complete sentence. Which of these shows the best word for Julie to use?

  Ⓐ "You knitted a sweater for my teddy, but it will fit him perfectly!"

  Ⓑ "You knitted a sweater for my teddy, and it will fit him perfectly!"

  Ⓒ "You knitted a sweater for my teddy, yet it will fit him perfectly!"

  Ⓓ "You knitted a sweater for my teddy, or it will fit him perfectly!"

17 At the start of sentence 31, Julie has not used verbs correctly. Which of these shows the correct way to write the sentence?

  Ⓐ My teddy bear be wearing that special sweater ever since, and he is always sitting proudly on my bed.

  Ⓑ My teddy bear being wearing that special sweater ever since, and he is always sitting proudly on my bed.

  Ⓒ My teddy bear has been wearing that special sweater ever since, and he is always sitting proudly on my bed.

  Ⓓ My teddy bear have been wearing that special sweater ever since, and he is always sitting proudly on my bed.

18 In sentence 32, Julie has not started the sentence correctly. Which of these shows the correct way to start the sentence?

  Ⓐ Whenever I see him, I think of Grandma and how much she wanted to do something special for me.

  Ⓑ Some time I see him, I think of Grandma and how much she wanted to do something special for me.

  Ⓒ Most of the time I see him, I think of Grandma and how much she wanted to do something special for me.

  Ⓓ Always I see him, I think of Grandma and how much she wanted to do something special for me.

END OF PRACTICE SET

Passage 9

In her physical education class, Jasmine was asked to write an opinion piece about something related to school life. She wrote about having healthy options at the school cafeteria. Read the opinion piece and look for any changes that should be made. Then answer the questions that follow.

Healthy Food At Our School

(1) We all want to be healthy so we can feel strong and enjoy life. (2) To be healthy it is important that we eat as much healthy food as we can. (3) Even though it can be very tempting, we should avoid eating junk food. (4) We also should try to eat lot of fruit and vegetable.

(5) The main reason all childs go to school is to learn new things. (6) Things we learn at school stay with us our whole lives. (7) I believe that at school, we should also learn to be healthy. (8) By having healthy and nutritious food choices at the cafeteria we will learn about healthy food. (9) We can also teach our friends and familys about healthy living.

(10) A big problem in the world is obesity. (11) There are many report's from scientists saying that junk food is contributing to this. (12) If we only serve healthy food, we am helping people to avoid obesity.

(13) If I eat healthy food at school, I can more concentrate. (14) If I eat bad food, I feel tired and lazy. (15) So, if we want to perform better at school and enjoy learning, I feel that eating healthy food is very important. (16) This is many harder to do when there is no healthy food available at school.

(17) Having healthy food at the cafeteria is not just about what we eat. (18) I believe that it will also teach us to think about other things that are good for us. (19) As an example, we may also think about getting more exercise. (20) Exercise is also important to stay fit and healthy. (21) At school we can learn to take a few minutes to think about our choices.

(22) It is very important that we have healthy food at our school cafeteria. (23) I feel that it could do a long-lasting difference to people's lives. (24) It would also set a good example. (25) Our students will be more healthy and more happy. (26) They will also continue to have good health for they're hole lives.

1 Which word in the title should NOT be capitalized?

- Ⓐ Food
- Ⓑ At
- Ⓒ Our
- Ⓓ School

2 Which of these shows where a comma should be placed in sentence 2?

- Ⓐ To be healthy, it is important that we eat as much healthy food as we can.
- Ⓑ To be healthy it is important, that we eat as much healthy food as we can.
- Ⓒ To be healthy it is important that we eat, as much healthy food as we can.
- Ⓓ To be healthy it is important that we eat as much healthy food, as we can.

3 In sentence 3, Jasmine wants to replace the word *should* with a word that makes it sound more important to avoid eating junk food. Which word would Jasmine be best to use?

- Ⓐ could
- Ⓑ may
- Ⓒ must
- Ⓓ can

4   Which of these shows the correct way to write sentence 4?

- Ⓐ   We also should try to eat lots of fruit and vegetable.
- Ⓑ   We also should try to eat lot of fruits and vegetables.
- Ⓒ   We also should try to eat lot of fruit and vegetables.
- Ⓓ   We also should try to eat lots of fruits and vegetables.

5   Which change should be made in sentence 5?

- Ⓐ   Replace *reason* with *reasons*
- Ⓑ   Replace *childs* with *children*
- Ⓒ   Replace *learn* with *learning*
- Ⓓ   Replace *new* with *knew*

6   Sentence 6 can be improved by adding a word to start the sentence. Which of these shows how to rewrite the sentence correctly?

- Ⓐ   A things we learn at school stay with us our whole lives.
- Ⓑ   To things we learn at school stay with us our whole lives.
- Ⓒ   The things we learn at school stay with us our whole lives.
- Ⓓ   Them things we learn at school stay with us our whole lives.

7 In sentence 9, what is the correct way to write *familys*?

- Ⓐ family's
- Ⓑ famillys
- Ⓒ families
- Ⓓ famillies

8 Which change should be made in sentence 11?

- Ⓐ Replace *There* with *Their*
- Ⓑ Replace *report's* with *reports*
- Ⓒ Replace *saying* with *said*
- Ⓓ Replace *this* with *these*

9 In sentence 12, *am* is not the correct word to use. Which of these shows the correct way to rewrite sentence 12?

- Ⓐ If we only serve healthy food, we is helping people to avoid obesity.
- Ⓑ If we only serve healthy food, we were helping people to avoid obesity.
- Ⓒ If we only serve healthy food, we will be helping people to avoid obesity.
- Ⓓ If we only serve healthy food, we has been helping people to avoid obesity.

10 Sentence 13 is not written correctly. Which of these shows the best way to rewrite the sentence?

- Ⓐ If I eat healthy food at school, better I can concentrate.
- Ⓑ If I eat healthy food at school, I better can concentrate.
- Ⓒ If I eat healthy food at school, I can better concentrate.
- Ⓓ If I eat healthy food at school, I can concentrate better.

11 Jasmine wants to add a sentence to the start of paragraph 4 to introduce the ideas in the paragraph. Which sentence would Jasmine be best to add before sentence 13?

- Ⓐ There should be a wide range of food choices to suit everyone.
- Ⓑ School days can feel very long and draining for many students.
- Ⓒ Teachers do not enjoy having students who are uninterested.
- Ⓓ Healthy food choices will also improve student performance.

12 In sentence 16, which word should replace *many*?

- Ⓐ more
- Ⓑ much
- Ⓒ most
- Ⓓ make

13 In sentence 19, Jasmine wants to replace the transition phrase with another phrase with the same meaning. Which phrase could Jasmine use?

- Ⓐ For instance,
- Ⓑ As a result,
- Ⓒ Above all,
- Ⓓ On the whole,

14 Which of these shows where the comma should be placed in sentence 21?

- Ⓐ At school, we can learn to take a few minutes to think about our choices.
- Ⓑ At school we can learn, to take a few minutes to think about our choices.
- Ⓒ At school we can learn to take a few minutes, to think about our choices.
- Ⓓ At school we can learn to take a few minutes to think about, our choices.

15 In sentence 22, Jasmine wants to replace "very important" with a single word with the same meaning. Which word should Jasmine use?

- Ⓐ crucial
- Ⓑ expensive
- Ⓒ supposed
- Ⓓ worthy

16 In sentence 23, which word should replace *do*?

- Ⓐ made
- Ⓑ make
- Ⓒ had
- Ⓓ been

17 Sentence 25 can be rewritten in a simpler way. Which of these shows the best way to rewrite the sentence?

- Ⓐ Our students will be healthier, happier.
- Ⓑ Our students will be more healthy happy.
- Ⓒ Our students will be healthier and happier.
- Ⓓ Our students will be healthier, happier too.

18 In sentence 26, the words *they're* and *hole* are both homophones. Which sentence uses the correct form of both homophones?

- Ⓐ They will also continue to have good health for their hole lives.
- Ⓑ They will also continue to have good health for there hole lives.
- Ⓒ They will also continue to have good health for their whole lives.
- Ⓓ They will also continue to have good health for there whole lives.

END OF PRACTICE SET

Passage 10

Lilly was asked by her history teacher to write a report on the first Moon landing. Read the report and look for any changes that should be made. Then answer the questions that follow.

The First Moon Landing

(1) Mankind first landed on the Moon on July 20 1969. (2) This was a big day in human history. (3) Mankind had been into space before, not to the Moon.

(4) The American President at that Time was John. F. Kennedy. (5) He had promised to get man to the Moon by the end of the 1960's. (6) He made that promise in 1961. (7) That day was fast approaching. (8) Many doubted if they would succeed in time.

(9) The successful mission was known as Apollo 11. (10) On the Apollo 11 mission were astronauts Neil Armstrong Buzz Aldrin and Michael Collins. (11) On the mourning of July 16, these three men lifted off from the Kennedy Space Center. (12) They left at 9:32 and just twelve minutes later were out of the Earth's atmosphere.

(13) Three days later, the crew were in the Moon's orbit. (14) A day after that, Armstrong and Aldrin got into the lunar module named *Eagle* and prepared for descent. (15) Collins remained in orbit in the control module named *Columbia*. (16) Armstrong and Aldrin success landed *Eagle* on the Moon's surface at 4:18 p.m.

(17) At 10:56 that evening, Armstrong was ready to climb out of *Eagle* and walk on the Moon's surface. (18) Around one billion people watched this event unfold on there television sets. (19) Armstrong climbed down the ladder and put his foot on the surface. (20) He famously said, That's one small step for a man, one giant leap for mankind.

(21) Aldrin then joined Armstrong on the surface of the Moon. (22) They spent two hours collecting samples. (23) In those two hours, they also took photos. (24) They put an American flag on the surface of the Moon. (25) Armstrong and Aldrin then returned to *Eagle*. (26) They blasted off, heading for the control module. (27) Collins was very excited to see them when they returned to *Columbia*.

(28) The full crew then returned to Earth. (29) They dropped into the pacific ocean near hawaii on july 24, 1969. (30) They had successfully landed on the Moon and returned safely. (31) Over the next three and a half years, more astronauts would make this journey. (32) Ten more would reach the Moon's surface. (33) The first Moon landing was an outstanding acheevement for scientists and engineers. (34) It paved the way for future space exploration.

1 Which of these shows the correct way to punctuate the date in sentence 1?

Ⓐ Mankind first landed on the Moon on, July 20 1969.

Ⓑ Mankind first landed on the Moon on July, 20 1969.

Ⓒ Mankind first landed on the Moon on July 20, 1969.

Ⓓ Mankind first landed on the Moon on July, 20, 1969.

2 As it is used in sentence 2, which word means about the same as *big*?

Ⓐ heavy

Ⓑ long

Ⓒ important

Ⓓ towering

3 In sentence 3, a word needs to be added after the comma to make a complete sentence. Which of these shows the correct word to use?

Ⓐ Mankind had been into space before, so not to the Moon.

Ⓑ Mankind had been into space before, and not to the Moon.

Ⓒ Mankind had been into space before, but not to the Moon.

Ⓓ Mankind had been into space before, for not to the Moon.

4 Which word in sentence 4 should NOT start with a capital?

- Ⓐ American
- Ⓑ President
- Ⓒ Time
- Ⓓ John

5 Lilly wants to add a word to the start of sentence 7 to create a better transition between sentences 6 and 7. Which of these shows the best transition word to use?

- Ⓐ Afterwards, that day was fast approaching.
- Ⓑ Mainly, that day was fast approaching.
- Ⓒ Surely, that day was fast approaching.
- Ⓓ Suddenly, that day was fast approaching.

6 Which of these shows how commas should be placed in sentence 10?

- Ⓐ On the Apollo 11 mission were astronauts Neil Armstrong Buzz Aldrin, and Michael Collins.
- Ⓑ On the Apollo 11 mission were astronauts Neil Armstrong, Buzz Aldrin, and Michael Collins.
- Ⓒ On the Apollo 11 mission were astronauts Neil Armstrong, Buzz Aldrin, and, Michael Collins.
- Ⓓ On the Apollo 11 mission were astronauts, Neil Armstrong, Buzz Aldrin, and Michael Collins.

7 Which change should be made in sentence 11?

- Ⓐ Replace *mourning* with *morning*
- Ⓑ Replace *these* with *them*
- Ⓒ Replace *men* with *man*
- Ⓓ Replace *Center* with *Senter*

8 Which of these shows where commas should be placed in sentence 12?

- Ⓐ They left, at 9:32 and just twelve minutes later, were out of the Earth's atmosphere.
- Ⓑ They left, at 9:32, and just twelve minutes later were out of the Earth's atmosphere.
- Ⓒ They left at 9:32 and, just twelve minutes later, were out of the Earth's atmosphere.
- Ⓓ They left at 9:32 and just twelve minutes later, were out of, the Earth's atmosphere.

9 In sentence 14, what is the correct way to spell *prepaired*?

- Ⓐ prepairred
- Ⓑ prepared
- Ⓒ preparred
- Ⓓ prepeared

10 In sentence 16, which word should replace *success*?

- Ⓐ successful
- Ⓑ successfully
- Ⓒ successes
- Ⓓ successness

11 Which change should be made in sentence 18?

- Ⓐ Replace *one* with *won*
- Ⓑ Replace *watched* with *watching*
- Ⓒ Replace *there* with *their*
- Ⓓ Replace *sets* with *set's*

12 Which of these shows how quotation marks should be used in sentence 20?

- Ⓐ "He famously said, That's one small step for a man, one giant leap for mankind."
- Ⓑ He famously said, "That's one small step for a man, one giant leap for mankind."
- Ⓒ He famously said, "That's one small step for a man," one giant leap for mankind."
- Ⓓ He famously said, That's one "small step" for a man, one "giant leap" for mankind."

13 In sentence 19, which word could replace *put* to suggest that he made the action gently?

- Ⓐ stomped
- Ⓑ shuffled
- Ⓒ placed
- Ⓓ poked

14 Lilly wants to combine the ideas in sentences 22 and 23. Which of these shows the best way to combine the sentences?

- Ⓐ They spent two hours collecting samples, and took photos.
- Ⓑ They spent two hours collecting samples also photos.
- Ⓒ They spent two hours collecting samples and taking photos.
- Ⓓ They spent two hours collecting samples, and took two hours taking photos.

15 In sentence 27, Lilly wants to replace "very excited" with a word with the same meaning. Which word could Lilly use?

- Ⓐ bothered
- Ⓑ dazed
- Ⓒ frustrated
- Ⓓ thrilled

16 Which of these shows the correct way to capitalize sentence 29?

- Ⓐ They dropped into the Pacific ocean near hawaii on July 24, 1969.
- Ⓑ They dropped into the pacific ocean near Hawaii on July 24, 1969.
- Ⓒ They dropped into the Pacific ocean near Hawaii on July 24, 1969.
- Ⓓ They dropped into the Pacific Ocean near Hawaii on July 24, 1969.

17 In sentence 33, what is the correct way to spell *acheevement*?

- Ⓐ achivement
- Ⓑ achevement
- Ⓒ acheivement
- Ⓓ achievement

18 In sentence 34, what does the phrase "paved the way" mean?

- Ⓐ educated
- Ⓑ prepared
- Ⓒ questioned
- Ⓓ smoothed

END OF PRACTICE SET

Passage 11

Penny was asked to write an essay describing her favorite subject at school. She prepared this essay for her teacher. Read the essay and look for any changes that should be made. Then answer the questions that follow.

My Favorite Subject At School

(1) My favorite subject at school is science. (2) In this essay, I will give the reasons for my choise.

(3) Science is a lot of fun. (4) I greatly enjoys all the experiments that we do in class. (5) We learn how to use special equipment and we look at many new and interesting things. (6) I am excited about going to high school, we will have even more equipment to use.

(7) I like science because we get to go outside and walk around the garden. (8) We find some specimens in the garden and observe the specimens under the microscope. (9) Bugs look fasinating under the microscope. (10) Sometimes we even go to the pond to catch aquatic bugs in our dip nets. (11) Being outside in the fresh air and being in nature with my friends is also enjoy.

(12) Our science teacher Mr. Hunter makes learning fun. (13) He always have interesting experiments prepared for us. (14) When he talks about science he gets very excited. (15) He helps us to appreciate the things we can seen around us every day. (16) He often organizes science craft projects too that are interesting. (17) I loved building a volcano from newspaper and painting it to make it look real.

(18) If you study science, there are a massive range of amazzing jobs and careers available to you. (19) As a result, I want to be an astronaut when I grow up. (20) If you want to be an astronaut, studying science is important. (21) Astronauts learn about space travel and how to take measurements in space.

(22) One day I would like to go to the Moon and maybe even go to Mars. (23) By the time I finish my education, travel to Mars could be possible. (24) I could be one of the first people to stand on Mars. (25) Wouldn't that be incredible.

(26) We get to watch many interesting videos in science class. (27) For example, I enjoy watching *Bill Nye the Science Guy* videos. (28) I always pay close attention to his videos because he explains scientific things in a simple weigh and I learn a lot. (29) Sometimes, I show these videos to my mom and dad when I get home from school and we discuss it together.

(30) School is great and I appreciate everything we learn. (31) My favorite subject is science. (32) My favorite subject is science because it has fun experiments, we get to go outside, our teacher is enthusiastic about science, there are amazing careers available, and I like watching science videos.

Science makes you really wonder about how the world works. It's exciting to learn the answers to so many questions.

1 Which word in the title should NOT be capitalized?

- Ⓐ Favorite
- Ⓑ Subject
- Ⓒ At
- Ⓓ School

2 In sentence 2, what is the correct way to write *choise*?

- Ⓐ chose
- Ⓑ choose
- Ⓒ choice
- Ⓓ chosse

3 Which change should be made in sentence 4?

- Ⓐ Replace *greatly* with *greater*
- Ⓑ Replace *enjoys* with *enjoy*
- Ⓒ Replace *experiments* with *experiment's*
- Ⓓ Replace *do* with *done*

4 In sentence 6, Penny needs to replace the comma with a word that connects the two clauses. Which of these shows the word that Penny should use?

Ⓐ I am excited about going to high school and we will have even more equipment to use.

Ⓑ I am excited about going to high school then we will have even more equipment to use.

Ⓒ I am excited about going to high school because we will have even more equipment to use.

Ⓓ I am excited about going to high school whether we will have even more equipment to use.

5 In sentence 8, Penny wants to avoid repeating the word *specimens*. Which pronoun could Penny replace "the specimens" with?

Ⓐ it
Ⓑ they
Ⓒ them
Ⓓ us

6 In sentence 9, what is the correct way to spell *fasinating*?

Ⓐ facinating
Ⓑ fasinateing
Ⓒ fascinating
Ⓓ fascinateing

7 In sentence 11, which word should replace *enjoy*?
- Ⓐ enjoyment
- Ⓑ enjoyable
- Ⓒ enjoying
- Ⓓ enjoys

8 Which of these shows how commas should be used in sentence 12?
- Ⓐ Our, science teacher, Mr. Hunter makes learning fun.
- Ⓑ Our, science teacher Mr. Hunter, makes learning fun.
- Ⓒ Our science teacher, Mr. Hunter, makes learning fun.
- Ⓓ Our science teacher, Mr. Hunter makes, learning fun.

9 In sentence 13, which word should replace *have*?
- Ⓐ has
- Ⓑ haves
- Ⓒ had
- Ⓓ hads

10 In sentence 15, which word should replace *seen*?

- Ⓐ saw
- Ⓑ see
- Ⓒ sees
- Ⓓ seeing

11 Sentence 16 can be rewritten to express the ideas more clearly. Which of these shows the best way to rewrite the sentence?

- Ⓐ He often organizes science craft projects too interesting.
- Ⓑ He often organizes interesting science craft projects too.
- Ⓒ He often organizes science craft projects interesting too.
- Ⓓ He often organizes science craft interesting projects too.

12 Which word in sentence 18 is spelled incorrectly?

- Ⓐ massive
- Ⓑ range
- Ⓒ amazzing
- Ⓓ available

13 In sentence 19, "As a result" is not the right transition phrase for the sentence. Which of these shows the best transition phrase to use to connect sentences 18 and 19?

- Ⓐ In summary, I want to be an astronaut when I grow up.
- Ⓑ In fact, I want to be an astronaut when I grow up.
- Ⓒ In the end, I want to be an astronaut when I grow up.
- Ⓓ In the meantime, I want to be an astronaut when I grow up.

14 Which sentence in paragraph 6 should end with a question mark?

- Ⓐ Sentence 22
- Ⓑ Sentence 23
- Ⓒ Sentence 24
- Ⓓ Sentence 25

15 Which change should be made in sentence 28?

- Ⓐ Replace *attention* with *atention*
- Ⓑ Replace *his* with *he's*
- Ⓒ Replace *weigh* with *way*
- Ⓓ Replace *learn* with *learned*

16 Penny wants to add the sentence below to paragraph 7.

> I enjoy chatting with them about all the things I have learned.

Where would Penny be best to place the sentence?

- Ⓐ After sentence 26
- Ⓑ After sentence 27
- Ⓒ After sentence 28
- Ⓓ After sentence 29

17 Which of these shows the best way to combine sentences 30 and 31?

- Ⓐ School is great and I appreciate everything we learn, so my favorite subject is science.
- Ⓑ School is great and I appreciate everything we learn, for my favorite subject is science.
- Ⓒ School is great and I appreciate everything we learn, but my favorite subject is science.
- Ⓓ School is great and I appreciate everything we learn, or my favorite subject is science.

18 In the caption at the end of the passage, which word would best replace the phrase "really wonder"?

- Ⓐ calm
- Ⓑ concerned
- Ⓒ confused
- Ⓓ curious

END OF PRACTICE SET

Passage 12

The students in Andrea's science class were asked to research an aquatic animal. Andrea wrote this report about jellyfish. Read the report and look for any changes that should be made. Then answer the questions that follow.

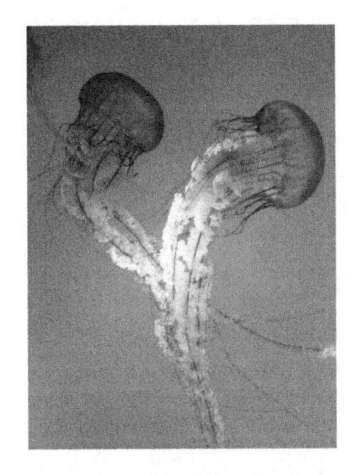

Jellyfish – Not Really Fish!

(1) Did you know that jellyfish have lived in the oceans for millions of years. (2) That is much more long than when dinosaurs first roamed the Earth! (3) Jellyfish are found in cold and warm water. (4) They like deep spots in the ocean and often live along coastlines. (5) Some jellyfish also live in fresh water seas.

(6) Jellyfish drift along the ocean currents. (7) They move forward when they squirt water from there mouths. (8) The mouth found underneath the bell-shaped main body. (9) It is surrounded by tentacles.

(10) The tentacles hang down from their bodies and are used for feeling and grasping. (11) The tentacles sweep the food towards their mouths. (12) Jellyfish like to eat fish, fish eggs, shrimp, crabs, and tiny sea plants. (13) Jellyfish can be eated by other larger jellyfish. (14) Sharks, swordfish, salmon, and sea turtles likes to eat jellyfish, too.

(15) Their tentacles have tiny stingy cells. (16) They can stun or paralyze prey. (17) The jellyfish stings can hurt humans. (18) However, its not that the jellyfish try to attack people. (19) Sometimes people are in the way and bump into a jellyfish in the water. (20) If the sting is from a dangerous species, the sting can be deadly. (21) One dangerous species that can be deadly is the box jellyfish.

(22) Jellyfish aren't really fish, some people call them jellies. (23) They are animals without backbones. (24) These animals are called invertebrates. (25) The jellyfish is not too smart. (26) It doesn't have a brain. (27) It doesn't have blood or a nervous system either. (28) It is made up of over 90% water.

(29) There are about 350 different kinds of jellyfish in the world. (30) Some jellyfish are clear and some are white, pink, yellow, blue, orange, red, green, purple, and multi-colored. (31) Depending on the kind of jellyfish, some live for just a few hours. (32) Others live for many years.

(33) The smallest jellyfish is the Creeping Jellyfish with a 0.5 millimeter body and short tentacles. (34) The largest jellyfish is the Lion's Main with a body of 2.3 meters and tentacles of 36.5 meters. (35) When jellyfish are together, they are called a bloom, swarm, or smack. (36) Sometimes, hundred of thousands of jellyfish can make up a group. (37) That's a lot of jellyfish!

Jellyfish sometimes travel in large groups of 100,000 or more creatures.

1 Which sentence in paragraph 1 should end with a question mark?

Ⓐ Sentence 1
Ⓑ Sentence 2
Ⓒ Sentence 4
Ⓓ Sentence 5

2 In sentence 2, which of these should replace "more long"?

Ⓐ more longer
Ⓑ more longest
Ⓒ longest
Ⓓ longer

3 Which change should be made in sentence 7?

Ⓐ Replace *move* with *moves*
Ⓑ Replace *squirt* with *squert*
Ⓒ Replace *there* with *their*
Ⓓ Replace *mouths* with *mouth's*

4 In sentence 8, Andrea needs to add a word after *mouth* to make a complete sentence. Which of these shows the word that Andrea should add?

- Ⓐ The mouth is found underneath the bell-shaped main body.
- Ⓑ The mouth are found underneath the bell-shaped main body.
- Ⓒ The mouth all found underneath the bell-shaped main body.
- Ⓓ The mouth be found underneath the bell-shaped main body.

5 In sentence 13, which word should replace *eated*?

- Ⓐ ate
- Ⓑ eat
- Ⓒ ated
- Ⓓ eaten

6 In sentence 14, which word should replace *likes*?

- Ⓐ like
- Ⓑ liking
- Ⓒ liked
- Ⓓ likely

7 Andrea wants to combine sentences 15 and 16. Which of these shows the correct way to combine the sentences?

- Ⓐ Their tentacles have tiny stingy cells, can stun or paralyze prey.
- Ⓑ Their tentacles have tiny stingy cells and do stun or paralyze prey.
- Ⓒ Their tentacles have tiny stingy cells that can stun or paralyze prey.
- Ⓓ Their tentacles have tiny stingy cells, ouch, can stun or paralyze prey.

8 Which change should be made in sentence 18?

- Ⓐ Replace *its* with *it's*
- Ⓑ Replace *try* with *trying*
- Ⓒ Replace *attack* with *atack*
- Ⓓ Replace *people* with *person*

9 Andrea wants to add the word *just* to sentence 19. Which of these shows the best place for the word?

- Ⓐ Sometimes just people are in the way and bump into a jellyfish in the water.
- Ⓑ Sometimes people just are in the way and bump into a jellyfish in the water.
- Ⓒ Sometimes people are just in the way and bump into a jellyfish in the water.
- Ⓓ Sometimes people are in the way just and bump into a jellyfish in the water.

10 Andrea wants to combine the ideas in sentences 20 and 21. Which of these shows the best way to combine the sentences?

Ⓐ If the sting is from a dangerous species, the box jellyfish, the sting can be deadly.

Ⓑ If the sting is from a dangerous species like the box jellyfish, the sting can be deadly.

Ⓒ If the sting is from a dangerous species, the sting can be deadly like a box jellyfish.

Ⓓ If the sting is from a dangerous species or a box jellyfish, the sting can be deadly.

11 Sentence 22 is not written correctly. Which of these shows a correct way to write the sentence?

Ⓐ Jellyfish aren't really fish, it's why some people call them jellies.

Ⓑ Jellyfish aren't really fish, that is why some people call them jellies.

Ⓒ Jellyfish aren't really fish, so why some people call them jellies.

Ⓓ Jellyfish aren't really fish, which is why some people call them jellies.

12 In sentence 25, *too* can be replaced with a better word. Which of these shows the best word to use?

Ⓐ The jellyfish is not much smart.

Ⓑ The jellyfish is not very smart.

Ⓒ The jellyfish is not more smart.

Ⓓ The jellyfish is not any smart.

13 Which of these shows the correct way to combine sentences 26 and 27?

Ⓐ It doesn't have a brain blood or a nervous system, either.

Ⓑ It doesn't have a brain blood, or a nervous system either.

Ⓒ It doesn't have a brain, blood, or a nervous system either.

Ⓓ It doesn't have a brain blood or, a nervous system, either.

14 A dictionary entry for the word *clear* is shown below.

> **clear** *adj*. 1. free from darkness 2. able to be seen through, colorless 3. easily seen 4. having a pure and even color

Which meaning of the word *clear* is used in sentence 30?

Ⓐ Meaning 1

Ⓑ Meaning 2

Ⓒ Meaning 3

Ⓓ Meaning 4

15 Andrea wants to add a transition phrase to the start of sentence 32. Which of these shows the best transition phrase to use?

Ⓐ In fact, others live for many years.

Ⓑ In the same way, others live for many years.

Ⓒ In the first place, others live for many years.

Ⓓ In contrast, others live for many years.

16 Andrea wants to add a transition phrase to the start of sentence 34. Which transition phrase would best connect the ideas in sentences 33 and 34?

- Ⓐ In addition,
- Ⓑ On the other hand,
- Ⓒ For instance,
- Ⓓ In other words,

17 Which change should be made in sentence 36?

- Ⓐ Replace *Sometimes* with *Sometime*
- Ⓑ Replace *hundred* with *hundreds*
- Ⓒ Replace *can* with *do*
- Ⓓ Replace *make* with *made*

18 Which word in the caption could be removed from the sentence and still have a complete sentence?

- Ⓐ travel
- Ⓑ groups
- Ⓒ more
- Ⓓ creatures

END OF PRACTICE SET

Passage 13

The students at Washington Elementary School were required to conduct a science experiment and then write a report for the annual science fair. Jon's experiment was on sunlight and plant growth. Read the report and look for any changes that should be made. Then answer the questions that follow.

Experiment: Sunlight on Plant Growth

(1) My experiment was to show if plants needs sunlight to grow. (2) First, I planted one bean seedling in each of the three pots. (3) The three seedlings were all the same size. (4) I watered the plants the same time, every day for three weeks. (5) I given each plant the same amount of water.

(6) One plant was placed in a dark closet. (7) The closet had no light. (8) Another plant was placed in a bedroom that had a little sunlight. (9) There was one large window that faced the south side of the house. (10) I closed the blinds part way during the daytime. (11) The third plant was placed near a living room window, did not have blinds or a curtain. (12) I also turned on a table lamp with a fluorescent bulb next the plant.

(13) Every day when I watered the plants, I messaged their height with a ruler. (14) I also marked down the color of each of the bean plants leaves. (16) I observed the growth of the stems. (17) After three weeks, I summarized the findings. (18) I will share these results.

(19) The bean plant that was placed by the open window grew the most. (20) Its leaves were the most large. (21) Its stems were wide and strong. (22) The plant was green and healthy. (23) The plant placed in the bedroom with a little light grew about half the size of the first plant. (24) Its leaves were light green and medium size. (25) The stems were more narrower than the first plant. (26) The plant that was in the dark closet grew the least. (27) The leaves were small and had yellow tips with brown edges. (28) Its stems were long and skinny.

(29) I learned from this experiment that all things need energy to grow. (30) Plants get there energy from sunlight. (31) This is called photosynthesis. (32) This means that the light is turned into food for the plants.

(33) So it seems that bean plants grow and change with the amount of light they receive. (34) They grow in size, thickness, and structure. (35) They turn different colors. (36) If there is fewer light, photosynthesis slows down. (37) Then the green color disappears and the leaves turn a lighter green, yellow, and even brown. (38) The stems don't grow as well.

(39) I learned a clear lesson from the experiment. (40) I now understand the importance of sunlight on plant growth. (41) Plants like all living things need energy to grow. (42) The more sunlight a plant receives, the larger it will grow.

1   Which change should be made in sentence 1?
   Ⓐ   Replace *My* with *Mine*
   Ⓑ   Replace *was* with *were*
   Ⓒ   Replace *needs* with *need*
   Ⓓ   Replace *grow* with *growing*

2   Sentence 4 is written incorrectly. Which of these shows a correct way to write the sentence?
   Ⓐ   I watered the plants at the same time every day for three weeks.
   Ⓑ   I watered the plants the same time, every day, for three weeks.
   Ⓒ   I watered the plants the same time, every day, and for three weeks.
   Ⓓ   I watered the plants for the same time every day for three weeks.

3   In sentence 5, which word should replace *given*?
   Ⓐ   give
   Ⓑ   gave
   Ⓒ   gived
   Ⓓ   gives

4 Jon wants to combine sentences 6 and 7. Which of these shows the best way to combine the sentences?

- Ⓐ One plant was placed in a dark closet with no light.
- Ⓑ One plant was placed in a dark closet, had no light.
- Ⓒ One plant was placed in a dark closet without no light.
- Ⓓ One plant was placed in a dark closet, closet had no light.

5 In sentence 11, Jon needs to replace the comma with a word to make a complete sentence. Which of these shows the change that Jon should make?

- Ⓐ The third plant was placed near a living room window that did not have blinds or a curtain.
- Ⓑ The third plant was placed near a living room window and did not have blinds or a curtain.
- Ⓒ The third plant was placed near a living room window there did not have blinds or a curtain.
- Ⓓ The third plant was placed near a living room window but did not have blinds or a curtain.

6 In sentence 12, which word should replace *next*?

- Ⓐ near
- Ⓑ nearer
- Ⓒ nearby
- Ⓓ nearly

7 In sentence 13, *messaged* is not the right word to use. Which word should Jon use?

- Ⓐ mastered
- Ⓑ metered
- Ⓒ measured
- Ⓓ managed

8 Which change should be made in sentence 14?

- Ⓐ Replace *also* with *all so*
- Ⓑ Replace *marked* with *marking*
- Ⓒ Replace *plants* with *plant's*
- Ⓓ Replace *leaves* with *leaf*

9 Jon wants to add a transition phrase to the start of sentence 16. Which of these shows the best transition phrase to use?

- Ⓐ Above all, I observed the growth of the stems.
- Ⓑ In addition, I observed the growth of the stems.
- Ⓒ All of a sudden, I observed the growth of the stems.
- Ⓓ In any event, I observed the growth of the stems.

10 In sentence 20, which word should replace "most large"?

Ⓐ largely
Ⓑ largest
Ⓒ larger
Ⓓ largeness

11 Jon wants to combine sentences 21 and 22. Which of these shows the best way to combine the sentences?

Ⓐ Its stems were wide and strong, and the plant was green and healthy.
Ⓑ Its stems were wide and strong, but the plant was green and healthy.
Ⓒ Its stems were wide and strong, yet the plant was green and healthy.
Ⓓ Its stems were wide and strong, nor the plant was green and healthy.

12 Which change should be made in sentence 25?

Ⓐ Replace *stems* with *stem's*
Ⓑ Replace *were* with *was*
Ⓒ Delete the word *more*
Ⓓ Replace *than* with *then*

13 In sentence 30, which word should replace *there*?

- Ⓐ them
- Ⓑ they
- Ⓒ their
- Ⓓ they're

14 Jon wants to rewrite sentence 33 by replacing "So it seems" with a transition phrase that sounds more certain and more serious. Which of these would NOT be a suitable way to start sentence 33?

- Ⓐ To sum up, bean plants grow and change with the amount of light they receive.
- Ⓑ As has been shown, bean plants grow and change with the amount of light they receive.
- Ⓒ In conclusion, bean plants grow and change with the amount of light they receive.
- Ⓓ There you go, bean plants grow and change with the amount of light they receive.

15 In sentence 36, *fewer* is not the right word to use. Which of these shows the correct word to use?

- Ⓐ If there is few light, photosynthesis slows down.
- Ⓑ If there is less light, photosynthesis slows down.
- Ⓒ If there is lesser light, photosynthesis slows down.
- Ⓓ If there is rare light, photosynthesis slows down.

16 Which of these shows a word that could be added to the end of sentence 38?

- Ⓐ The stems don't grow as well either.
- Ⓑ The stems don't grow as well never.
- Ⓒ The stems don't grow as well neither.
- Ⓓ The stems don't grow as well ever.

17 Which of these shows the correct way to place commas in sentence 40?

- Ⓐ Plants, like all living things need energy, to grow.
- Ⓑ Plants like all, living things need energy, to grow.
- Ⓒ Plants, like all living things, need energy to grow.
- Ⓓ Plants like, all living things, need energy to grow.

18 Which sentence from the last paragraph would be the best caption for the illustration at the end of the passage?

- Ⓐ Sentence 39
- Ⓑ Sentence 40
- Ⓒ Sentence 41
- Ⓓ Sentence 42

END OF PRACTICE SET

Passage 14

Marybeth's language arts teacher asked her students to write about a person in history. Marybeth wrote a report about Amelia Earhart. Read the report and look for any changes that should be made. Then answer the questions that follow.

Amelia Earhart – The Woman Who Loved to Fly

(1) Amelia Earhart was born on July 24 1897. (2) She had a younger Sister named Muriel. (3) The girl's lived with their grandparents when they were young. (4) Then the girls went to live with their mother in Chicago.

(5) Amelia studied nursing. (5) After that, she went to live with her parents in California. (6) Her father took her to an air show. (7) This is where she done her first ride in an open-cockpit plane.

(8) Amelia took flight lessons in California. (9) She became a pilot. (10) She purchased her first plane. (11) It was yellow so she called it "The Canary." (11) Amelia enjoyed flying and breaking records. (12) She breaked a record for flying above 14,000 feet.

(13) Once she was a passenger in a flight across the Atlantic. (14) She wanted to make the trip just she. (15) In 1932 she finally got her wish! (16) She began her journey to cross the Atlantic Ocean. (16) She became the first woman to fly solo across the Atlantic Ocean. (17) She then planned a trip around the world. (18) She crashed during take off. (19) When her plane was repaired, she tried again.

(19) This time, Amelia and a co-pilot set off to fly around the world. (20) They flew to Puerto Rico and towards Africa. (21) Then the Middle East and Australia. (22) They then flew to New Guinea. (22) Now the plane had flew 22,000 miles and had just 7,000 miles left to go.

(23) Right after the plane left New Guinea, she sent several call for help. (24) But she could not hear the return messages on her radio. (25) The plane was off course. (26) It was running out of gas over the Pacific Ocean. (27) It's not known exactly what happened, but they were never scene or heard from again. (28) President Roosevelt sent nine naval ships and 66 aircraft to search for her. (29) Eventually, the search was called off.

(30) To this day, exactly what happened to Amelia Earhart remains a mistery. (31) Some people say her plane crashed in the ocean. (32) Others say that she was taken prisoner by people living on the Pacific Islands. (33) The truth may never be known for sure. (34) However, Amelia Earhart will always be remembered as a brave woman who loved to fly!

1 Which word in the first paragraph should NOT be capitalized?

- Ⓐ July
- Ⓑ Sister
- Ⓒ Muriel
- Ⓓ Chicago

2 Which of these shows the correct way to punctuate the date in sentence 1?

- Ⓐ Amelia Earhart was born on July, 24 1897.
- Ⓑ Amelia Earhart was born, on July 24, 1897.
- Ⓒ Amelia Earhart was born on, July, 24 1897.
- Ⓓ Amelia Earhart was born on July 24, 1897.

3 Which change should be made in sentence 3?

- Ⓐ Replace *girl's* with *girls*
- Ⓑ Replace *their* with *there*
- Ⓒ Replace *grandparents* with *grandparent's*
- Ⓓ Replace *were* with *was*

4 In sentence 7, which word should replace *done*?

- Ⓐ had
- Ⓑ have
- Ⓒ went
- Ⓓ gone

5 Marybeth wants to rewrite sentence 11. Which of these shows the best way to rewrite the sentence?

- Ⓐ "The Canary," she called it, because it was yellow.
- Ⓑ It was yellow, so "The Canary" she called it.
- Ⓒ She called it "The Canary" because it was yellow.
- Ⓓ It was called "The Canary" and so it was yellow.

6 In sentence 12, which word should replace *breaked*?

- Ⓐ break
- Ⓑ breaks
- Ⓒ broke
- Ⓓ broken

7 In sentence 14, "just she" is not the best phrase to use. Which word would best replace "just she"?

- Ⓐ ourself
- Ⓑ oneself
- Ⓒ herself
- Ⓓ yourself

8 Which change should be made in sentence 15?

- Ⓐ Add a comma after *1932*
- Ⓑ Replace *got* with *gotten*
- Ⓒ Replace *finally* with *finaley*
- Ⓓ Replace the exclamation point with a question mark

9 Marybeth wants to add a transition word to the start of sentence 18. Which of these shows the transition word that best links sentences 17 and 18?

- Ⓐ Suddenly, she crashed during take off.
- Ⓑ Unfortunately, she crashed during take off.
- Ⓒ Certainly, she crashed during take off.
- Ⓓ Lastly, she crashed during take off.

10 In sentence 22, "had flew" is not the correct verb tense. Which of these shows the correct way to write the sentence?

Ⓐ Now the plane had flied 22,000 miles and had just 7,000 miles left to go.

Ⓑ Now the plane had flown 22,000 miles and had just 7,000 miles left to go.

Ⓒ Now the plane have flew 22,000 miles and had just 7,000 miles left to go.

Ⓓ Now the plane have flown 22,000 miles and had just 7,000 miles left to go.

11 Which sentence in paragraph 5 is not a complete sentence?

Ⓐ Sentence 19

Ⓑ Sentence 20

Ⓒ Sentence 21

Ⓓ Sentence 22

12 Which change should be made in sentence 23?

Ⓐ Replace *Right* with *Write*

Ⓑ Replace *left* with *leave*

Ⓒ Replace *several* with *sevaral*

Ⓓ Replace *call* with *calls*

13 In sentence 24, the words "could not" can be shortened. Which of these shows the correct way to shorten the words?

- Ⓐ coul'dnt
- Ⓑ could'nt
- Ⓒ couldn't
- Ⓓ couldn't'

14 In sentence 27, Marybeth has made an error and used the wrong homophone for one of the words. Which change should be made to correct the error?

- Ⓐ Replace *It's* with *Its*
- Ⓑ Replace *not* with *knot*
- Ⓒ Replace *scene* with *seen*
- Ⓓ Replace *heard* with *herd*

15 Marybeth wants to add the sentence below to paragraph 6.

> Despite all the people looking, there was no sign of her or her plane.

Where would be the best place for the sentence?

- Ⓐ After sentence 26
- Ⓑ After sentence 27
- Ⓒ After sentence 28
- Ⓓ After sentence 29

16 Which word in sentence 30 is spelled incorrectly?

- Ⓐ exactly
- Ⓑ happened
- Ⓒ remains
- Ⓓ mistery

15 Marybeth wants to combine sentences 31 and 32. Which of these shows the best word to use to combine the sentences?

- Ⓐ Some people say her plane crashed in the ocean, them others say that she was taken prisoner by people living on the Pacific Islands.
- Ⓑ Some people say her plane crashed in the ocean, when others say that she was taken prisoner by people living on the Pacific Islands.
- Ⓒ Some people say her plane crashed in the ocean, then others say that she was taken prisoner by people living on the Pacific Islands.
- Ⓓ Some people say her plane crashed in the ocean, while others say that she was taken prisoner by people living on the Pacific Islands.

18 In sentence 33, which word could replace *sure*?

- Ⓐ certain
- Ⓑ firm
- Ⓒ false
- Ⓓ clear

END OF PRACTICE SET

Passage 15

Sun Young wrote a letter to the principal asking him to consider allowing the students to have a morning healthy snack break. Read the letter and look for any changes that should be made. Then answer the questions that follow.

Healthy Snack Break – Why Not?

Dear Principal Jordan

(1) I think that it would be a good idea to allow a morning snack break. (2) Many students get up early to get to school. (3) Some kids catch the bus as early as 6 o'clock. (4) Others may eat breakfast an hour or more before they get to school. (5) Still others may not have time to have breakfast or even feel like eat that early in the morning.

(6) As you know, the lunch break is at Midday at the moment. (7) This is a long time to wait to eat. (8) I think kids feel better when they wasn't hungry. (9) I think they can learn better, too. (10) We have learned in health class that eating healthy foods throughout the day is good for us bodies. (11) And since kids have smaller stomachs they get full fast. (12) That's why kids need to eat more often.

(13) I would like you to seriously consider adding a morning healthy snack break to our dayly routine. (14) I know that many schools have a morning snack break, and it's a grate thing for those schools. (15) You could have a break any time. (16) I think before or after morning recess might be a good time.

(17) You could also encourage healthy eating by having a healthy snack break. (18) In fact, you might even require eating only healthy snacks. (19) For example, fruits, vegetables, whole grains, and low-fat dairy products make healthy snacks. (20) And low-fat milk, water, soy drinks, and fruit juices are healthy beverages. (21) Also, kids could brainstorm healthy snacks with their teachers to better know what foods to brought for the snack break.

(22) I don't think that the healthy snack break would interrupt learning. (23) Overall, it will actually help kids to stay focused. (24) Students will have more concentration. (25) They won't be thinking about lunch so much. (26) They won't feel hungry and be in a bad mood because of it. (27) They will learn more about healthy eating and the importance of eating foods full of nutrients. (28) In the end, kids will also be able to learn more in their subjects.

(29) Thank you muchly for considering my request. (30) I hope to hear from you soon.

(31) Sincerely,

Sun Young Kim

Students would be able to concentrate better if we had a healthy snack break.

1 The greeting of the letter is missing punctuation. Which of these shows the correct way to punctuate the greeting?

Ⓐ Dear Principal Jordan.

Ⓑ Dear Principal Jordan,

Ⓒ Dear Principal Jordan –

Ⓓ Dear Principal Jordan:

2 Which sentence in paragraph 1 would be best to end with an exclamation point?

Ⓐ Sentence 1

Ⓑ Sentence 2

Ⓒ Sentence 3

Ⓓ Sentence 4

3 In sentence 5, which word should replace *eat*?

Ⓐ eats

Ⓑ eaten

Ⓒ eating

Ⓓ ate

4 Which change should be made in sentence 6?

Ⓐ Replace *know* with *no*

Ⓑ Replace *is* with *are*

Ⓒ Replace *Midday* with *midday*

Ⓓ Replace *moment* with *momant*

5 In sentence 7, Sun Young wants to add a word to emphasize how long the wait is. Which of these shows the correct word to add?

Ⓐ This is a terrible long time to wait to eat.

Ⓑ This is a terribly long time to wait to eat.

Ⓒ This is a terribleness long time to wait to eat.

Ⓓ This is a terriblesome long time to wait to eat.

6 In sentence 8, which contraction should replace *wasn't*?

Ⓐ weren't

Ⓑ aren't

Ⓒ isn't

Ⓓ didn't

7 In sentence 10, *us* is not the correct pronoun to use. Which of these shows the correct pronoun to use?

- Ⓐ We have learned in health class that eating healthy foods throughout the day is good for them bodies.
- Ⓑ We have learned in health class that eating healthy foods throughout the day is good for our bodies.
- Ⓒ We have learned in health class that eating healthy foods throughout the day is good for my bodies.
- Ⓓ We have learned in health class that eating healthy foods throughout the day is good for their bodies.

8 Which of these shows the correct place to add a comma in sentence 11?

- Ⓐ And since, kids have smaller stomachs they get full fast.
- Ⓑ And since kids, have smaller stomachs they get full fast.
- Ⓒ And since kids have smaller stomachs, they get full fast.
- Ⓓ And since kids have smaller stomachs they get, full fast.

9 Which word in sentence 13 is spelled incorrectly?

- Ⓐ seriously
- Ⓑ consider
- Ⓒ dayly
- Ⓓ routine

10 Which change should be made in sentence 14?

- Ⓐ Replace *have* with *having*
- Ⓑ Replace *it's* with *its*
- Ⓒ Replace *grate* with *great*
- Ⓓ Replace *those* with *them*

11 Sun Young wants to rewrite sentence 17. Which of these shows the best way to rewrite the sentence?

- Ⓐ Having a healthy snack break could also encourage healthy eating.
- Ⓑ Encourage healthy eating, a healthy snack break could.
- Ⓒ You could encourage healthy eating, also, by having a healthy snack break.
- Ⓓ A healthy snack break, by having, could also encourage healthy eating.

12 Sun Young wants to rewrite sentence 20 so it does not start with the word *and*. Which of these shows a correct way to rewrite the sentence?

- Ⓐ Healthy beverages always low-fat milk, water, soy drinks, and fruit juices.
- Ⓑ Healthy beverages offer low-fat milk, water, soy drinks, and fruit juices.
- Ⓒ Healthy beverages is low-fat milk, water, soy drinks, and fruit juices.
- Ⓓ Healthy beverages include low-fat milk, water, soy drinks, and fruit juices.

13 In sentence 21, which word should replace *brought*?

- Ⓐ bring
- Ⓑ brings
- Ⓒ bringer
- Ⓓ bringing

14 In sentence 23, *Overall* is not the best transition word to use. Which of these shows the best transition word to use?

- Ⓐ Somewhat, it will actually help kids to stay focused.
- Ⓑ Likely, it will actually help kids to stay focused.
- Ⓒ Instead, it will actually help kids to stay focused.
- Ⓓ Otherwise, it will actually help kids to stay focused.

15 Sun Young wants to combine sentences 24 and 25. Which of these shows the best word to use to connect the sentences?

- Ⓐ Students will have more concentration although they won't be thinking about lunch so much.
- Ⓑ Students will have more concentration because they won't be thinking about lunch so much.
- Ⓒ Students will have more concentration whenever they won't be thinking about lunch so much.
- Ⓓ Students will have more concentration besides they won't be thinking about lunch so much.

16 Sun Young can simplify sentence 26 by replacing "be in a bad mood" with a single word. Which of these shows the correct word to use?

- Ⓐ They won't feel hungry and crusty because of it.
- Ⓑ They won't feel hungry and creepy because of it.
- Ⓒ They won't feel hungry and crafty because of it.
- Ⓓ They won't feel hungry and cranky because of it.

17 Sun Young wants to change the end of sentence 27 to express the ideas in a simpler way. Which of these shows the correct words to use in place of "foods full of nutrients"?

- Ⓐ They will learn more about healthy eating and the importance of eating nutrientable foods.
- Ⓑ They will learn more about healthy eating and the importance of eating nutrientful foods.
- Ⓒ They will learn more about healthy eating and the importance of eating nutrientment foods.
- Ⓓ They will learn more about healthy eating and the importance of eating nutritious foods.

18 In sentence 29, *muchly* is not the right word to use. Which of these is a correct way to write the sentence?

- Ⓐ Thank you so much for considering my request.
- Ⓑ Thank you too much for considering my request.
- Ⓒ Thank you more much for considering my request.
- Ⓓ Thank you any much for considering my request.

END OF PRACTICE SET

ANSWER KEY

Passage 1

1. D	7. C	13. D
2. C	8. B	14. A
3. A	9. B	15. B
4. B	10. A	16. B
5. A	11. C	17. D
6. B	12. C	18. B

Passage 2

1. D	7. B	13. B
2. C	8. C	14. B
3. B	9. C	15. B
4. D	10. C	16. D
5. A	11. B	17. C
6. C	12. A	18. D

Passage 3

1. A	7. A	13. C
2. B	8. B	14. D
3. D	9. A	15. B
4. C	10. A	16. A
5. C	11. B	17. C
6. D	12. C	18. A

Passage 4

1.C	7.D	13.B
2.B	8.C	14.A
3.A	9.C	15.B
4.D	10.A	16.D
5.D	11.B	17.C
6.C	12.B	18.A

Passage 5

1.A	7.A	13.D
2.D	8.D	14.C
3.A	9.D	15.A
4.D	10.B	16.B
5.D	11.B	17.D
6.C	12.C	18.C

Passage 6

1.B	7.D	13.D
2.C	8.D	14.D
3.A	9.C	15.A
4.B	10.C	16.D
5.D	11.C	17.C
6.D	12.A	18.D

Passage 7

1. B	7. B	13. D
2. A	8. D	14. D
3. D	9. B	15. B
4. C	10. C	16. C
5. D	11. B	17. B
6. B	12. C	18. A

Passage 8

1. D	7. C	13. B
2. B	8. C	14. D
3. C	9. B	15. B
4. B	10. B	16. B
5. B	11. C	17. C
6. D	12. C	18. A

Passage 9

1. B	7. C	13. A
2. A	8. B	14. A
3. C	9. C	15. A
4. D	10. D	16. B
5. B	11. D	17. C
6. C	12. B	18. C

Passage 10

1.C	7.A	13.C
2.C	8.C	14.C
3.C	9.B	15.D
4.C	10.B	16.D
5.D	11.C	17.D
6.B	12.B	18.B

Passage 11

1.C	7.B	13.B
2.C	8.C	14.D
3.B	9.A	15.C
4.C	10.B	16.D
5.C	11.B	17.C
6.C	12.C	18.D

Passage 12

1.A	7.C	13.C
2.D	8.A	14.B
3.C	9.C	15.D
4.A	10.B	16.B
5.D	11.D	17.B
6.A	12.B	18.D

Passage 13

1. C	7. C	13. C
2. A	8. C	14. D
3. B	9. B	15. B
4. A	10. B	16. A
5. A	11. A	17. C
6. A	12. C	18. D

Passage 14

1. B	7. C	13. C
2. D	8. A	14. C
3. A	9. B	15. C
4. A	10. B	16. D
5. C	11. C	17. D
6. C	12. D	18. A

Passage 15

1. B	7. B	13. A
2. C	8. C	14. C
3. C	9. C	15. B
4. C	10. C	16. D
5. B	11. A	17. D
6. B	12. D	18. A

Get to Know Our Product Range

Mathematics

Practice Test Books
Practice sets and practice tests will prepare students for the state tests.

Quiz Books
Focused individual quizzes cover every math skill one by one.

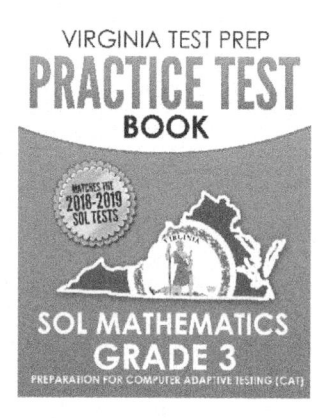

Reading

Practice Test Books
Practice sets and practice tests will prepare students for the state tests.

Reading Skills Workbooks
Short passages and question sets will develop and improve reading comprehension skills.

Writing

Writing Skills Workbooks
Students write narratives, essays, and opinion pieces, and write in response to passages.

Persuasive and Narrative Writing Workbooks
Guided workbooks teach all the skills required to write effective narratives and opinion pieces.

Language

Language Quiz Books
Focused quizzes cover spelling, grammar, writing conventions, and vocabulary.

Revising and Editing Workbooks
Students improve language and writing skills by identifying and correcting errors.

Language Skills Workbooks
Exercises on specific language skills including idioms, synonyms, and homophones.

http://www.testmasterpress.com

Made in the USA
Columbia, SC
19 October 2021